THE

MAKING

OF A

FRINGE

CANDIDATE

1992

THE MAKING OF A FRINGE CANDIDATE 1992

BY LENORA B. FULANI

Castillo INTERNATIONAL

Castillo International, Inc.
500 Greenwich Street, Suite 201
New York, New York 10013

Library of Congress Catalog Number: 92-76223

Fulani, Lenora B.
The Making of a Fringe Candidate — 1992

ISBN 0-9628621-3-4

TYPOGRAPHY BY ILENE ADVERTISING, NEW YORK
BOOK DESIGN BY DAVID NACKMAN AND ILENE HINDEN
COVER DESIGN BY GARY BARBER

97   96   95   94   93   5   4   3   2   1

Manufactured in the United States of America

CONTENTS

Preface

It's the morning after Election Day, and I'm sitting in my Harlem office trying to take everything in…It is somewhat mind-boggling to think that I am personally acquainted with Bill Clinton, the next president of the United States — and that he's not exactly crazy about me!

It's been an exhausting, exhilarating, absolutely incredible year and a half! More than ever before, I feel that I'm part of the historic process that's taking place in our country and worldwide — when clearly the political landscape is undergoing a seismic change.

I feel very strongly the emotional impact of having a hand in shaping history…I am so moved, and thrilled, and humbled. Because although the "pundits" are insisting that independent politics is a "lost cause," that there will never be a third party in America, the American people have apparently decided otherwise. And for the last ten years I have been working as hard as I know how to influence them in that independent direction.

I feel very responsible for those people who follow independent leadership, and tremendous love for their courage and their willingness to seem ridiculous for doing so. They are electoral revolutionaries.

I think the 1992 presidential election was the most important election of the late 20th century. The American electorate "Just Said No" to the nakedly anti-poor, pro-Big Business economics of right-wing Republicanism and put a Democrat in the White House for the first time in 12 years. But voters are becoming sophisticated — they weren't simply counting on the Democratic Party to come through for them: Of the 65% who said NO! to the reactionary Republican Party, 20 million voters said YES! to Ross Perot (the well-known independent), to me, to Andre Marrou, to Dr. John Hagelin and the other independent presidential candidates. This year saw the largest independent vote in U.S. history — lots of folks said no to the two-party system.

The American people made it clear that they won't be taken in again by a self-serving Democratic Party whose leaders have nothing against the spoils system as long as they get their "fair share" of the spoils! There's a new force in U.S. politics — the American people — who have proven that they are ready, willing and able to create and hold on to some political leverage for themselves, even while giving the Democrats a mandate for change. The American people have finally figured out that voting independent (not for the Republicans) is the way to put pressure on the Democratic Party.

Now, to put it crudely, the Democrats have to put up or shut up. And, with almost 20% of the electorate voting on November 3 for an independent presidential candidate, independent politics has taken a giant leap forward. My role — as always — is to make sure that the Black community, the Latino community, the lesbian and gay community, the poor, rank-and-file labor and women will all be a vital force in defining and shaping that movement.

Although this was a landmark year for the independent political movement, those who rule America and those who speak for them are desperate for the rest of us to believe that the two-party system through which they exercise power is the "natural state" of American politics.

That's why, whenever genuinely independent political movements have appeared on the horizon, all-out efforts were

made to destroy them, first by coopting their leaders. If that
didn't work, the leaders were discredited, vilified, and demo-
nized. When all else failed, they were murdered. Because of the
pivotal role that the working-class Black community plays in
such movements, independent Black leaders have always been
regarded by the powers-that-be as a particular threat: Malcolm
X, Dr. Martin Luther King, Jr., the Black Panther Party. (Those
who resisted cooptation in life are sometimes more "coopera-
tive" dead; once buried, they may be safely resurrected as mon-
uments — and lucrative ones, at that.)

To me, the really shocking and frightening thing about all
this isn't that the powers-that-be view independent Black
leaders as dangerous and respond to us accordingly — for
them to act otherwise would be out of character. What I find
much more disturbing is the sordid role that some "respectable" Black leaders have played in this drama: a lot of
Black leadership stood by silently while the gunsights were
trained on Malcolm after he had plainly moved to the left.
When Dr. King took a public stand against the war in
Vietnam, many Black leaders publicly dissociated themselves
from him. In the late '60s the Communist Party and others
on the "official" (white Democratic Party-approved) left used
their token Black leaders to cast orthodox Marxist aspersions
on the revolutionary Black Panthers. In all three cases the
message was, "They are not one of ours. They are too far left.
Do whatever you want to them." The rulers of America were
given to understand that they could get away with murder —
and they did.

In 1992, virtually no Black leader spoke out in my defense
against the smear campaign waged by Ron Daniels and his
cronies on the official "left" — a campaign which had COIN-
TELPRO written all over it.

Bruce Shapiro, writing in the *Nation*, a flagship publication of the American liberal/left, called the movement I am building a "snake-oil show" and urged the IRS to investigate me. Michael Tomasky, writing about the New Alliance Party — which I chair — in the *Village Voice*, said, "the point...is to kill it."

Despite official denials, there is documented evidence to show that NAP has been under continuous investigation by the FBI since my 1988 presidential campaign; internal Bureau documents at one time identified NAP as "armed and dangerous." Virtually no Black leader has publicly condemned this anti-Constitutional attack on the movement that I lead.

During the New York primary, when the sudden death of Congressman Ted Weiss meant that the NAP-backed candidate who was challenging him might become the next congressman from his predominantly Jewish district on the upper west side of Manhattan (there was no one else on the ballot), the political establishment from Governor Mario Cuomo down — including Mayor David Dinkins and the Manhattan borough president, Herman "Denny" Farrell, both of whom are Black — went into overdrive to persuade voters that the dreaded New Alliance Party must be defeated at all costs. They were backed up by primary day editorials in every daily newspaper. But not one Black leader in New York stood up for NAP (not to mention democracy, not to mention me!).

Back in 1985, when David Dinkins (he was then the Manhattan borough president) obediently mounted the steps of City Hall to tell Minister Louis Farrakhan to stay out of New York, I held a press conference to welcome the Minister to the city. I was there for Louis Farrakhan.

In 1991, when the cops stood aside and let a potential assassin stab the Reverend Al Sharpton — who at the time was not the media favorite he is today, with over 160,000 Democratic Party votes under his belt, but a political "untouchable" as far as the official Black leaders were concerned — I was there for Al Sharpton.

I've been there for every Black leader in this country who's come under attack.

What I don't know is where *they* are now that the guns are fixed on me — when silence could mean death.

A lot of people didn't speak up for Malcolm, or for Dr. King, or for the Panthers, because it simply wasn't expedient for them to do so: it would have made them look bad; it could have been embarrassing or awkward; it might have cost them a job, or a congressional seat, or their status as a "respectable" Black leader.

I'm not saying that other Black leaders need to vote for me or campaign for me or endorse any of my ideas. I don't necessarily see eye to eye with all of the sisters and brothers for whom I have stood up. However, agreement isn't what's needed. The point is that I'm one of those on the front lines now and — so far — Black leaders are leaving me out there alone.

But history is most definitely not over! It will show where all of us stand, and on whose side.

Over the last year I shaped this book from a series of extended conversations I had with Phyllis Goldberg, a journalist and friend, in the heat of the 1992 presidential campaign. We talked late at night, early in the morning, in person and over the phone, whenever I could grab a couple of hours. I've tried to share, as honestly as possible, my impressions of and insights into that whole very complicated process as it was going on. In doing so, my intention was not to be hurtful to anyone, but to open up some of the issues that I think are of real concern to the American people.

— **LENORA B. FULANI**
New York City, November 4, 1992

ACKNOWLEDGEMENTS

All of my love and thanks to my family in Chester, Pennsylvania; my children, Ainka and Amani; the extraordinarily dedicated organizers (their names could fill a book!) who have worked side by side with me over the last 13 years to build the independent New Alliance Party; and of course the people, from Coos County in northern New Hampshire to the Castro in San Francisco, who have had the courage, the decency and the independence of mind to stand with me and say to the powers-that-be: "We're proud to be fringe!" I love you all.

My deepest appreciation to the slightly smaller group of people at Castillo International who helped to make *The Making of a Fringe Candidate — 1992:* Gary Barber for his beautiful cover; Ilene Hinden and David Nackman, like Gary very talented designers, who are responsible for the book's good looks; my loving and lovely friends and colleagues, Gabrielle Kurlander, my publisher, and Jacqueline Salit, both of whom read and reread the manuscript with such scrupulous attention; Phyllis Goldberg, my longtime editor and speechwriter, who spent a year with me writing this book and who was so easy to talk to; Dan Friedman, an activist journalist in the best sense of both words, who asked the tough questions that helped to produce "Pro-Gay 365 Days a Year"; Michael Klein, the brilliant "answer man" who found the dates and the quotes and checked the facts; Freda Rosen, the managing editor and Kim Svoboda, the traffic coordinator, who together made sure

everything came in on schedule; my friend and Castillo's pro-
duction manager extraordinaire, Diane Stiles, who always gets
the job done; Margo Grant, Kate Henselmans, Jessica Marta,
Jessica Massad, Jeff Roby, Richard Ronner, Lauren Ross, Alice
Rydel and Chris Street, the hardworking proofreaders who got
it all right; Madelyn Chapman, my very talented press secretary;
and Candice Sherman and Bob Levy, whose business expertise
shaped the book from the start.

I am grateful in advance to Thecla Farrell, Roger Grunwald,
Donna Kaseta, Michael Klein, Tara Lewis, Lisa Linnen, Elaine
Mannheimer, Michelle McCleary, Arthur Rubin and Pat Wictor,
the Castillo International workers responsible for distributing
this book by any means necessary.

I am honored by the kind words of Claude Brown and
Eugene McCarthy, and deeply touched by Debra Olson's warm
introduction: the feelings are mutual!

My heartfelt thanks, love and appreciation go to Fred
Newman, my campaign manager and closest friend, without
whom there would have been no fringe candidate.

INTRODUCTION

"Debra Olson, you keep the strangest company!" my highly successful political activist friend from the Democratic Party commented to me as I waved goodbye to Dr. Lenora Fulani after the recent National Gay and Lesbian Task Force Seminar in Los Angeles.

"What do you mean?" I asked rather naively.

"Debra, the woman stands on chairs! Once I saw her standing on a chair, shouting about injustice to this very influential and important group of people."

"Well," I responded, "maybe we should have all joined her and this world wouldn't be in such a mess!"

Yes, Lenora Fulani stands on chairs! She also screams her message from the back of flatbed trucks which roll slowly through the poor communities of urban America. But just when you think you have this most unusual woman figured out, she appears magnificently dressed for an important political dinner and speaks with presidential eloquence and clarity the same words she has been "shouting from the chairs and in the streets." These are the words of freedom, honesty and responsibility, the words that, in 1992, became the cry of Independent Politics. Grassroots organizations and ordinary citizens throughout the country spent much of 1992 rejecting the two-party political system that rewarded greed and incompetence and supported the "good ol' boy" network, and leadership emerged to answer the need for new alternatives. Ross Perot

certainly gained the most attention, but other, incredibly im-
passioned men and women also seized the opportunity to speak
out against the dehumanizing "babble of bureaucracy." Dr.
Fulani was one of them.

The language of Dr. Fulani is the language of the streets. It
is the language of vision and compassion. She touches in each
of us a common chord and has helped us face our deepest fears
by speaking about them frankly and honestly. Fulani addresses
our rage and articulates our real feelings and thoughts.

We are at a crucial moment in the evolution of humankind.
Fear and ignorance keep us separated and pitted against one another. This is a carefully calculated strategy, orchestrated by the
power brokers to create separation and division, thus disem-
powering us. It is up to our leaders to bring together the great-
est minds and hearts who want to be of service by helping to facilitate the conscious awakening of all individuals, organizations
and countries. The time is now for the social and economic
transformation that will lead us into the 21st century. Getting
America back on the right course will require frank and honest
dialogue among leaders and the public on what is wrong and
how to repair the damage before it is too late.

Ross Perot called to action over 25 million mostly white
middle-class Americans. Add to this the countless disenfranchised, women, people of color, gays and lesbians who heard
the call to action of Dr. Fulani. Then include those who responded to the intelligent call for creative solutions to today's
most serious problems as articulated by Dr. John Hagelin, the
presidential candidate of the Natural Law Party. The sheer di-
versity of these three remarkable candidates showed in micro-
cosm the power and enlightenment which is possible.

Dr. Lenora Fulani's part in the process of this past election
was to keep EVERYONE honest. She comes from the heart no

matter what the message. During my early involvement with the Perot movement I was struck by the incredible momentum and spirit of the "grassroots" movement.

After Mr. Perot's sudden withdrawal from the race I focused my efforts on helping to forge a coalition of viable third-party alternatives so that this energy did not dissipate with the sudden "disappearance" of one leader. We tried to reach out to Mr. Perot, as you will read in Dr. Fulani's chapter on him, but he and at least some in the "United We Stand" organization chose not to advance the cause of the independent movement in a coalitional direction.

I will never forget the morning Orson Swindle, Ross Perot's national campaign manager, called me from his car phone on the way to the first presidential debate. I had been very aggressively attempting to arrange a meeting in Dallas with Mr. Perot and Dr. Fulani, Dr. Hagelin and Mr. Andre Marrou, the Libertarian Party's presidential candidate, to discuss the development of a strong coalition to open up the system and give the American people more choices. Orson proceeded to tell me that he wouldn't recommend a meeting because he wasn't sure what personality their "party" was going to develop! This comment absolutely confused and frustrated me.

In the early stages of Mr. Perot's campaign I found him to be completely open and available to "the people," as witnessed by his statements and posture at the two meetings (one in Orange County, the other in Dallas) that he had with representatives of national gay and lesbian leaders. He certainly did not in any way fit the mold of the right-wing "redneck" candidate in which some had tried to cast him. However, after his withdrawal and subsequent re-entry into the campaign, it seemed that most of the key individuals who remained involved in the effort to elect Perot spent most of their time battling one another for prestigious positions instead of getting on with the business of building strong coalitions of grassroots power to bring about change. I've been told this is natural in the early stages of a new movement. However it saddened me deeply because we have so little time to reform our corrupt political system and policies, as well as to address the impending economic and environmental disasters that confront us.

I prefer to give Ross the benefit of the doubt. He not only created great excitement during the election year, he awakened the activist spirit within millions of Americans. However, when Ross Perot says he belongs to the American people — the "grassroots" — he'd better realize that's US! *ALL* OF US!

As you'll see, Dr. Fulani and others worked hard to reach out to and align the various movements in an attempt to empower the people of this country, but they were all ignored by the higher-ups in the Perot campaign. However, I continue to hope, as I watch this grassroots network expand even beyond the election, that it will have a life of its own. It was with a sense of great optimism that I observed Dr. Fulani take the podium at a "United We Stand" Perot event at the Los Angeles Convention Center and win the hearts and minds of this disenchanted and now basically "leaderless" group of intelligent activists. They were mesmerized and inspired by her intelligence and vision. Her innocence, on the one hand, her belief that the truth must be told and that people do want to hear that truth no matter how painful, and her uncanny ability on the other hand to "paint a picture" of the importance of real people having a voice in the matters that touch their lives, were enough to make this group continue to believe that they could and would be involved in changing "politics as usual." I watched Dr. Fulani become a "beacon of light" to these Perot patriots and empower them, as surely as she has to countless others who have been blessed with the opportunity to hear her speak.

I love this woman with all my heart. She's what I call a "light bearer." Her courageous moves against the world of "established politics" continue to fuel the myth surrounding her. She is unflinchingly honest and her articulate method of communicating real issues about real people leaves nothing questionable about her mission or agenda. No one leaves a Fulani speech wondering what she meant! I smile inwardly when I reflect how she "pushes everyone's buttons." It is painfully evident that racism and sexism are alive and well and run deep in the American psyche. To watch Dr. Fulani break down these old ideas and archaic belief systems is part of the genius of this extraordinary woman.

After meeting with her for the first time in New York I knew that Lenora Fulani would be critical to the formation of the citizen-action coalition which is now being developed as a result of all these powerful networks of concerned citizens coming together. I felt an immediate responsibility to introduce her to people who, like myself, had never met her, and, even more importantly, to those who had formed shallow and preconceived opinions of this woman and what she and the New Alliance Party represented. Most of these beliefs, I later discovered, were a result of the "political establishment" creating a false persona for her in an attempt to disempower and discredit her. The scenario that continuously repeated itself was that even people who had heard of Dr. Fulani or had the opportunity to see her on C-Span, CNN or "Crier and Company" and thought they knew what she was about came away with a new vision of her and an undeniable respect for her power and credibility.

We have forgotten what it is like to have leaders who will truly lead and speak the truth instead of deceiving us with empty promises of gain without pain and continued harvest without hardship. I applaud the leadership and incredible courage of Dr. Lenora Fulani. She has compelled us to recognize on both a conscious and subconscious level the plight of minorities — something which will be felt, to the great benefit of our children, for many generations to come. All young people can look to the vision of limitless possibilities she represents. She should be celebrated for breaking the mold of the traditional white male presidential candidate, and she should be honored for providing a wake-up call to the nation at large on many levels.

We have very little time left to turn around the destiny of this planet and her people. I hope and pray that we see and hear more of Dr. Lenora Fulani in the months and years to come and that each of us may show the courage it takes to "stand up on that chair and scream" along with her.

— **DEBRA OLSON**
Beverly Hills, CA, December 1992

1

THE FIRST SHOTS

State Democratic Chairman Chris Spirou has said the scene in Nashua won't be repeated. "Some of us in New Hampshire have smelled the gunpowder of battle before," he said. "If they think they are going to intimidate Chris Spirou with these tactics, they're sadly mistaken."

— *CONCORD MONITOR*, DECEMBER 30, 1991

When Larry Agran (the former mayor of Irvine, California and another "minor" presidential candidate) and I made our way onto the stage at the first Democratic Party primary presidential debate in Nashua, New Hampshire (we were uninvited), it was something else. I was fine, I guess, but everything was moving so fast. I knew that I needed to get up there. I didn't mind fighting with the Democratic Party powers-that-be (including Spirou). I was mostly concerned with making a strong political statement. I thought I'd have more time. My pocketbook was in the car, with every note I had ever taken. I forgot all about health care (that's what the forum was about) — except that we the people needed it and we didn't have it.

I started out by saying, "I do have a new dress, but I didn't wear it because I wasn't invited here." I said who I was. I introduced people in the audience from Harlem. I thanked Doug

Wilder, the governor of Virginia, one of the "Big Six" Democrats, for giving up some of his time so that I could speak. Jay Rockefeller, the senator from West Virginia who was acting as moderator, growled at me for speaking too long. I said, "I'm not the timekeeper — you are."

It was nerve-racking. There were fights going on all over the place. One of Rockefeller's assistants kept harassing me. Wilder was whispering in my ear. I don't remember what he was saying. At one point he told me I could share his mike. Thanks, Doug.

At first, having succeeded in getting into a presidential debate after four years of trying, I felt enormous pressure to do something brilliant. It was awful, because I couldn't think. Then I got a note from my campaign manager, Fred Newman. He told me not to get carried away attacking the Democrats because in this situation — the Democratic Party primary — I was one! So I calmed down. I loved it when Larry Agran did what he did. Someone said, "Get her off the stage!"

Larry said, "I don't even know her!" Then the cops started to move — it was intense.

I had the clear *experience* of being in a club — a Democratic Party men's club. In retrospect, I think that after I spoke I should have left the stage and gone back to sit with the audience. I don't like to be in a position where they — the men's club — can project that they're giving me something, or doing me a favor.

The audience response afterward was good. I felt like a warrior for the people. A white working-class man came up and apologized for the way I had been treated. One man said he was ashamed and it would never happen again. A white working-class woman hugged me. It was clear that after Rockefeller and the rest of the Democrats told Larry Agran and me to get off the stage and I said "no," they didn't know what to do. Our posture was: We're *in* the debates. Now they have to throw us out. That's democracy!

Defiant followers of the New Alliance Party shut down an address by Bill Clinton at Harlem Hospital yesterday, frustrating the presidential candidate's efforts to campaign among New York blacks.

Standing on her chair, an angry Lenora Fulani attacked Clinton's behavior toward blacks and demanded to know why fringe candidate Larry Agran was not included in upcoming Democratic debates.

— NEW YORK *DAILY NEWS*, MARCH 29, 1992

Clinton is mighty arrogant. I applauded him outside as he was walking into the hospital. I grabbed his hand and wouldn't let go. He smiled but wouldn't say anything. That's his modus operandi. Then we went into the lobby and started chanting "WE WANT AGRAN." That got to him a little. I stood up because I realized that would be the most disruptive — he could not avoid me. I was intent on having him respond. I was saying to him that he can't just dis, ignore, avoid Black folks. He had a responsibility to be inclusive.

I also knew he wasn't going to take questions. I wanted to convey that our people aren't intimidated by him — and if we are, we're going to move ahead anyway. I knew I wasn't going to let him talk and that C. Virginia Fields, the city council-woman from Harlem, and the other Black Democrats who were hosting Clinton didn't have enough moral authority to shut me up. I didn't know what he was going to do, but I knew I wasn't going to let him finish his speech unless he answered my question — "Why won't you let Larry Agran into the debates?"

It never dawned on me that it would be so symbolic of how many people in the Black community feel about Clinton. I didn't think the media would touch it. I was trying to figure out what would be the best way to force this man to pay attention to what the people of Harlem and I had to say to him. And it worked.

Every Black woman spends her life trying to avoid being related to as a Black bitch. A lot of what it means to fight in this rumble is being willing to look like a Black bitch or to be related to as one. It means giving up hesitancy, and the need for validation. It freaks people out — including the Black working class. They're comfortable, even if they're dying, with my being Black and mellow, or a beautiful African queen, or whatever. But this outspoken Black woman stuff is shaking them up.

Three cops were injured last night in a scuffle when 150 protesters tried to force their way into the auditorium where the presidential debate was being held, police said. The demonstrators included New Alliance Party presidential candidate Lenora Fulani.

— NEW YORK POST, APRIL 1, 1992

The cops beating me up at Lehman College summed up the beginning stage of the presidential campaign in '92. At Harlem Hospital and at Lehman, people's reactions to me were stronger than before. Some liked it a lot — an older Black woman came up to me at an event soon afterward and said, "I saw your man the other night!" She meant Clinton. She was tickled.

But I've also been angry at the Black community. If I had

gotten killed at Lehman that night, I would have been a martyr in 20 seconds and forgotten a week later. Black people need to be challenged to support leaders, even if they're female, while we're alive. I'm demanding that they do something other than memorialize me.

What happened at Lehman was hardly an isolated incident. I have felt the hatred toward us very strongly. Part of what it means to come to be more human is that you feel this hatred more. Before I had felt it in how people related to Reverend Sharpton and Minister Farrakhan. Part of my growth is feeling that hatred, that venom, directed at me. The ugliness of the establishment is real...they're out to get us. And that ain't paranoia. Regular racism — the ordinary garden variety of crazy white people — I'm used to. The hostility of the Black establishment toward me — I'm making it hard for them and they hate us and I embody what they hate — is new.

I've gotten much more popular support than ever before. But I also got more hate mail in the two weeks after Harlem Hospital than ever. People were livid. Some of it (it seems to me) had to do with my being a Black working-class woman who was doing working-class things. Lots of people want me to be more middle-class. There are rules for how to be a spokesperson — you don't stand on chairs, you don't curse. You act like a lady.

I'm having a lot of reactions to what I'm doing. As Che said, it's risking seeming ridiculous. It's being willing to step out of roles, and into other roles. Some days I go to fancy dinners, sometimes I stand on chairs and yell.

What happened at Harlem Hospital made me aware of how close we are to power. Bill Clinton and Jerry Brown were so silly, so undistinguished, it was hard to keep in mind that they were running for the presidency of the U.S.A. I feel like I came to know them in ways that stripped them of anything that's intimidating to me. It's not like challenging David Dinkins — I stood on a car and yelled at him for 20 minutes when he was running for mayor in 1989 and I was "dogging" him all over the city. But David Dinkins was not the Democratic Party's handpicked candidate for president of the United States. Bill Clinton was, and I was able to run him out of that room, out of Harlem. That must have gotten to some folks. That's why the cops were willing to rough me up at Lehman — they didn't have to. People have come out more, showing their dirty hands.

Rev. Jackson has set Jan. 25 for a meeting in Washington, D.C., at the Omni Shoreham Hotel, where he and other key members of the movement have invited the Democratic candidates to be quizzed on a variety of domestic and foreign issues.

However, Dr. Lenora Fulani, an African-American candidate for the presidency and a New York resident, who recently received federal matching funds far exceeding the amount obtained by some of the other contenders, was not invited to Washington by Rev. Jackson and company.

—NEW YORK *AMSTERDAM NEWS*, JANUARY 4, 1992

Jesse's changed, history's changed, I've changed. So my feelings have changed. It makes me sad sometimes.

The first time I heard Jesse Jackson speak in person was in February of 1987, when he was the keynote speaker at the Black and Puerto Rican Legislative Caucus weekend in Albany. He was magnificent, brilliant, stunning. Michael Hardy, an activist attorney, journalist and a political colleague, introduced us. I spoke to Jesse at the Rainbow Coalition breakfast the next morning. I had stood up and spoken about our "Two Roads" plan — supporting Jackson's quest for the Democratic Party presidential nomination and then (in the likely event that he would not be the party's standard bearer) making an independent run for the presidency so that the millions of people who supported him would not be abandoned in the general election — and said that we were looking for an independent presidential candidate. Jesse's response was very warm and open. He said that we needed to keep all our options open. And he had his picture taken with me.

We met next in Detroit, at a labor rally organized by Congressman John Conyers. We both addressed the rally. Then I walked into the room where he was holding a press conference and he called out, "Bring it to me, Fulani!" It was sexual. It was disarming. It threw me. I thought it was inappropriate. It seemed unpresidential. I didn't know quite how to respond. And my discomfort opened up for me the whole issue of sex and politics.

I used to have the experience a lot of being attacked in public, viciously attacked, by Black men, particularly elected officials, who afterward would hit on me in private. I couldn't understand it — I wondered why, if they were politically unsupportive, they were coming on to me. Pretty naive, huh? I would be furious at them for what they were saying about Black people, about poor people. Of course men use coming on to you as a weapon. I took offense at Jesse coming on like that. I thought, This is not how you greet me, politically.

Male politicians are allowed to be flirtatious and sexual in public. I don't have to be passive sexually, stuck in my role as a proper woman. I've worked hard to break out of that role, to be sexual and intimate in public as a Black woman political leader.

The next time I saw Jesse was a few months later in North

Carolina. His whole demeanor toward me had changed. You could feel the chill from the stage. I ran up and threw my arms around him and said, "Hi, Jesse! It's so great to see you!" I told him that one of his people, a Rainbow Coalition person, had canceled an event to prevent me from speaking at it. Jesse's response was, "I had nothing to do with it." He was beginning to realize that I wasn't just this cute babe in the woods — that I was seriously pursuing the independent road.

Part of the experience of 1987 and 1988 was of running after Jesse. I was enormously proud of him. I remember the rage I felt when I found out how he had learned that Michael Dukakis had offered the vice presidential slot to Lloyd Bentsen. Even so, attack after attack came from Black Democrats and members of the Rainbow Coalition, who said that I was hurting Jesse. At the same time there was an enormous response from the community to the Two Roads plan. I was willing to take the heat, but I also had strong reactions to it.

So we had a strange relationship. I was finally coming to realize that Jesse Jackson was a Democrat, and that I had the high ground relative to his campaign. NAP's posture was that the Black community, not the Democratic Party, had produced Jesse Jackson. And that he was ours, not theirs.

It finally dawned on me late in 1991 that Jesse simply wouldn't talk to me and there was something very wrong with that. Where does he get off? It's not a personal statement about me — that I'm not pretty enough, or charming enough — it's a political statement about our community. He's selling out the Black Agenda.

I want to have a public dialogue with him. I don't feel intimidated by him as I used to. I've been able to take it out of the personal arena. I want him to come to the table. He owes that to our people. I'd be thrilled if that happened.

The difference between me and Jesse has gotten clearer to everyone. You could *see* it during the 1992 campaign. Clinton was with Jesse, insulting the Black community. You didn't see Clinton with me — except when I was running him out of Harlem Hospital.

Rainbow Coalition people called up when I was on a radio talk show in Pittsburgh to attack me. They're doing Jesse's dirty work. One caller said, "She bashes Black men." But I'm not bashing Black men. I'm bashing white politics.

Feminist author Gloria Steinem last night dismissed the popular notion that 1992 is the "year of the woman," saying that there are too few women in Congress and that too many men remain hostile to woman candidates.

— *SAN FRANCISCO CHRONICLE*, SEPTEMBER 9, 1992

So much work goes into everything we do. The women who ran for office in 1992 as Democrats — they plugged into places that already existed. All they had to do was show up. For progressive independents there's a whole other level of energy and work involved — like going into the California Peace and Freedom Party and being related to as the crazy left, and going into Black leadership meetings and being related to as a "fringe" Black leader.

I'm learning how to live with the contradiction of doing very important things for which you get almost no credit.

Barbara Powell, the president of the Hempstead, Long Island NAACP chapter, was trying to get me into the presidential forum at the NAACP's national convention. She worked very hard to do this and at one point in the process she expressed her concern that I not "bogart" the NAACP. I told her the issue was how come she wouldn't bogart them with me —

I'll take whatever chances are necessary for Black people, for all people.

She told me that she thought more people would support me but they didn't have the balls and that she was going out on a limb for me. "Thank you," I said. "You should."

She also told me that the reason the National Organization for Women didn't invite me to their presidential forum was that I gave Molly Yard (NOW's former president) a stroke! Presumably Molly had a two-year delayed reaction to the fight we had in 1988, when — at the NOW convention in Buffalo — she tried to grab a microphone out of my hands and I wouldn't let go. I have a lot of fights, working-class fights.

You can't fight politely for freedom. This is not a white-glove affair.

2

CAMPAIGNING FROM NEW HAMPSHIRE TO CALIFORNIA

After Jesse Jackson decided not to run for president, Lenora Fulani decided to step in and take his place.

Fulani, who ran as a third party candidate in 1988, filed papers to appear on the New Hampshire Democratic ballot yesterday. She promised to bring voters a message of connection — to show New Hampshire residents that they have more in common with poor black people in inner cities than politicians would have them believe.

— *CONCORD MONITOR*, DECEMBER 18, 1991

The first time I campaigned at The Mall of New Hampshire was in December of 1991. I was anxious more than scared. I'm usually in situations where there are at least *some* Black people. But this time JoAnne, my aide, was the only Black person there besides me! So I knew I had to stretch.

It's hard to go into a mall four days before Christmas, when people are shopping, and campaign. But once I got started it was fine. I knew things were going well when the store owners started running around madly. The initial thing was jumping in and getting it rolling.

I had no idea what white folks in New Hampshire were going to say. I didn't think they were going to say terrible things.

If I had thought about it, I would have expected that they weren't going to take me seriously. But they did! Talking to young white people was like talking to Black working-class youth — they were so serious and decent. It took a very short period of time to realize that it was the same. The majority of people are polite. They'll stop. And we would connect.

We've been talking for a long time about projecting NAP's multi-racial politics. I've always felt that I needed to do it better. This was a real opportunity to provide leadership to white folks — to touch them.

That New Hampshire experience has had a real impact on how I organize in the Black community. I feel able to articulate a class politic better. I feel less dependent on the Black community. It's very liberating. It frees me up to say things to the Black community that I haven't been able to. I think it's more a posture than that I know new words. It's a class posture. I'm saying to the Black community that what I'm about is working people, middle-class people, all people.

In some ways I felt less encumbered up there — unencumbered by the weight of bad Black leadership. It felt like you could move mountains. People related to me as a human being and a leader, rather than a stereotype. That's something. Except for white folks I trust because I work with them and know them, I hadn't taken that big a risk — to reach out to ordinary white folks.

It's not like I didn't experience racism up there. But I didn't let it stop me. What I was doing was climbing over racism and saying, "Okay, let's see what we can do with some of the people who are being racist." Some people may look at you with a sneer, but you just go right through that and talk to them. I think that's critical: if we can't build in the presence of racism, or in the presence of sexism, we're up the creek. Because that's what there is. We're teaching Black people that you can't stop because somebody's racist to you. You have to figure out what to do with that. And that's a very valuable lesson.

The white working-class communities have responded to our message. It's real, it connects with what's actually happening in the world. Being able to reach these folks comes out of 15 years of collective work. A woman wearing a button for Bob Kerrey — the Nebraska senator who was one of the so-called "Big Six" in the primary — came up to me and said how much she liked what I was doing. Then the issue became how to turn that response into a vote, how to bring people like her into the independent democracy movement.

I was the major figure at the forum in Berlin up in Coos County, New Hampshire where only the minor candidates showed up. And I think I would have been even if all the "majors" had come. Some party officials in the state started saying to me, "It's a privilege to have you here." They were somewhat hesitant, somewhat scared, but they were saying it.

There was so much pain in people's eyes. A 76-year-old man came up to me in a restaurant and said, "I don't want to interfere with your lunch…but I'm in so much pain. I feel so lost. I don't think you have an answer, but I'm so old, and so low, that I'm willing to come to you."

I learned not to take that as an insult. What else could he think? The white working class was reaching out to me through all the garbage. That must be very frightening to the powers-that-be, to the degree that they can even know what's going on.

The experience of strangers falling in love with me — it was so intimate — I felt turned on all the time. I was saying, "I just want to participate with you in changing what's going on." People have been so insulted by America's political leaders, you almost don't want to talk with them, to touch the level of depression, of emptiness, in their lives.

Clinton was touring a fishery. All he could think of to say to a man who was in danger of losing his job was, "What kind of fish is this?" Politicians act as if people are fools.

Democratic presidential candidate Dr. Lenora Fulani told students at Daniel Webster College on Tuesday that America is no longer a democracy and the seven major candidates, which she called "murderers, villains and crooks," will continue to strip Americans of their rights…"The real thing to be pissed-off about is the big leaguers spitting in our faces," Fulani said. "They just keep spitting and spitting. And why wouldn't they, we just keep voting them into office."…Freshman Beth Cummings, 19, was "impressed" with Fulani. "This is the first time I felt like I wasn't being lied to," Cummings said. "She is a person for the people."

— *THE TELEGRAPH* [NASHUA, NH], JANUARY 29, 1992

Part of my connection to young people is my idealism. Also, I experienced a lot of pain in my life as a kid, or watching kids I was close to be in pain that I couldn't do anything about. I started crusading at a very early age to save my nieces and nephews. There were people I knew intimately as decent human beings who were destroyed before the age of ten. I think that had a real impact on me. One of the worst things to watch is the destruction of the kind of idealism, the kind of hope, that kids have. I can't think of anything that's more of an inspiration than to create a world in which they're able to build decent lives. I like their truthfulness — they don't have time for phonies, which I deeply appreciate.

I was blown away by the white kids up in New Hampshire, and I think they were blown away by me. There was a huge difference between me and the "Big Five" (the ones who were left after Doug Wilder dropped out), and a lot of the other minor candidates wouldn't spend time with the kids. But I thought it was important that I make a statement by being there. It's great that they learned that they have other options now, before they're old enough to vote, and that they can do something about "the system."

In Holderness, which is up in the White Mountains, I spoke to fifth, sixth, seventh and eighth graders. At first they were sitting and looking at me. And I was looking at them, thinking, What in the world can we do together? I said to them, "I'm supposed to tell you things that sound like your textbooks. I'm not going to. I want to talk to you about the real world, and what politics really is, and what your responsibility is to change that." Then I talked to them about democracy. And they heard it. They were touched by it, they responded. I think young people pick up on real things.

Black and Latino youth are regarded as a vast and profitable market for every manner of entrepreneur — white and Black — looking to make a buck off our kids' love of music. Overselling tickets and underspending on security preparations disrespect our children and create an environment where our kids are literally set up to die. The problem isn't, as some commentators say, the rap scene. It's the rip-off scene in which our young people become concert cattle in the hands of grown-up entrepreneurs who don't have the human decency to put safety above the almighty dollar.

— FROM MY STATEMENT PROTESTING THE DEATHS OF EIGHT YOUNG PEOPLE AT A RAP CONCERT ON THE CAMPUS OF THE CITY COLLEGE OF NEW YORK, DECEMBER 1991

I like rap a lot. Living with two teenagers (my kids!), I have to! My feelings about rap music are even stronger than how I felt about break dancing, and I liked that a lot. I'm moved by how enterprising young Black kids are. They don't have access to bands to play for them, so they've created music that doesn't need a band. Some Black jazz musicians I've known put down rappers. They think rap isn't "real" music. I think rap's very creative. Adults need to support it. Some rap I like, some rap I find ridiculous, and some rap offends me. But I still support it, because I support our young people. It's their generation's love songs. I don't think rap as a form of rebellion can change our society on its own. In fact, some of the most militant raps are really just written to make a buck for record companies. Rap music, to me, is a way our young people are figuring out how to be part of our mixed-up society.

I defend 2 Live Crew and Professor Griff of Public Enemy when they are censored. Bill Clinton's attack on Sister Souljah, the rapper, was just a cowardly way of attacking Black youth. Even if you disagree with our young people, you have to support them first. Then maybe you can reach them, learn from them and have them learn from you. The playing field of life is so grossly tilted against them — they have nothing — that you can't just attack these youth when you disagree.

What concerned me most about the controversy surrounding Ice-T and his rap "Cop Killer" is that the police don't respond when police officers *murder* our people as strongly as they respond to anti-cop lyrics in a rap song. The police have a lot of nerve to be offended because kids turn their justifiable outrage about police brutality into rap lyrics.

I once had a good fight with Doug E. Fresh, the rap star. I was trying to get him to endorse our voter registration drive in 1990 and he wouldn't because he didn't want to be associated with my campaign. Doug E. said he didn't know enough about what I represented and that someone had told him I was a communist. I said all he had to do was stand on any street corner in Harlem, ask people who I was and he'd find out. I told him that "fight the power" was hypocritical; it was just rhetoric unless you support those of us who *are* fighting the power. I asked him why he cared if I was a communist. It was an intense dialogue. I think he was a little taken aback. I really respect Doug E. He's supported young people, and works to be a good role model for them. I think he could come out even more! We've stayed in touch.

DALLAS, July 16—In halting his campaign before it ever formally began, Ross Perot explained today that the Democratic Party had become so much stronger recently that he no longer believed he could win the election at the polls in November.

— *NEW YORK TIMES,* JULY 17, 1992

Running for president of the United States as a Black woman (with no money, to boot) shows I'm not easily daunted! I wasn't surprised when Perot pulled out, but I was enraged. I was enraged at his arrogance, his complete disregard and disdain for his supporters. Thirty million mostly white Americans put themselves on the line for him. I was very impressed with them.

For all the revolutionary rhetoric I hear in Harlem, the middle-class and working-class white community beat the Black community to independent politics. They moved to support Perot and said, "Goodbye Democratic and Republican Parties." They showed that they're ready to do something radical to benefit America. They left the Black community in the dust.

For California's Peace and Freedom Party, founded in 1967 to become one of the only two ballot-status socialist parties in the country, this year was a chance to talk about unity and alternatives to "politics as usual," despite even a lot of bitter divisions within their own party.

Over 200 delegates and another 200 observers gathered in San Diego last weekend to choose their Presidential candidate from two Black independent candidates, Lenora B. Fulani and Ron B. Daniels.

Though Fulani carried the majority of votes in the primaries, winning 50% or 4,215 votes while Daniels won only 32.5% or 2,690 votes, the final decision rested with the delegates, who chose Daniels over Fulani with 120 to 96 votes.

This reversal, and the tensions at the convention, reflected in much fighting within the Party.

— *Observer* [California], August 20, 1992

Before the Peace and Freedom Party convention, I called 300 Peace and Freedom delegates. They were taken aback. They couldn't believe that I'd call them since they knew that I knew that they hated NAP. Nevertheless, I was calling to tell them, "If you're a delegate, you're a leader. People are looking to the Peace and Freedom Party for leadership. There are moves to make so we can do something together." Reaching out to them was very powerful.

Black people often have a knee-jerk reaction to white leftists: you don't have to respect them.

The convention was an exercise in discipline. It meant staying in there with people, not allowing ourselves to get provoked when our opponents acted crazy. The temptation was to say, "I'm not taking this! You want to be crazy, be crazy on your own." But who would benefit? Not independent politics. I was making a unity statement. I was practicing inclusiveness. I felt as if I'd been sent to "leftist school." I was going in and providing leadership. It would have been easier to stay in the Black community — that's for sure!

All of us working inside Peace and Freedom had been sectarian. But there was a political openness in '92 and the left had the chance to do something big. We couldn't blow that for petty reasons, like someone had said "Fuck you" to someone else three years ago. The left, despite its *mishegas,* has held on to a progressive social vision. It has to be embraced for that. Even though Maureen Smith, then the Peace and Freedom Party chairperson, was supporting Ron Daniels as the party's presidential nominee, I worked with her. I invited her to participate on a panel on independent politics at our NAP convention, which was held later in the summer.

And I was teaching the leftists in Peace and Freedom: Tell us your progressive history, so the African American working-class people here know why we're in the same room together. We can't come together if you're yelling "cult!" at us from across the room.

During that time I was also talking to my supporters — many of them working-class and middle-class white women who weren't leftists — who told me that they'd been looking for me all their lives. Their passion was so enormous — I could barely have those conversations without weeping.

A man from our hardcore opposition said to me, "The people who you registered in Peace and Freedom aren't real socialists." Of course he was right. They're working people.

I organized each of my supporters to go to the convention as a coalition member of a pluralistic party, who didn't get provoked, who was putting out a pro-Peace and Freedom Party message. Because that's what we were.

I expressed my concern to Maureen Smith that Ron Daniels hadn't been building the Peace and Freedom Party. And he hadn't unified the party. By yelling "cult" and "guru" — this is what he called NAP and my campaign manager Fred Newman — he'd insulted Peace and Freedom registrants who voted for me and who were activists in the party. The presidential candidate of Peace and Freedom had to speak for the whole party, I told Maureen, which included the people who voted for me. Since she was the chair of the *whole* party, I reminded her, she had to guarantee that when Daniels got up to speak he didn't attack members of our party.

Back in 1988, the Peace and Freedom convention was very negative. It was a mess — so much so that it ended up with no presidential candidate, even though people — including me — were running. The convention was so undemocratic that I walked out with dozens of my supporters and held another convention. The secretary of state ruled that there would be no Peace and Freedom Party candidate because no "duly convened convention" was held. Maureen told me that the 1988 convention was the worst political experience of her life. I said that was reason enough not to repeat it!

Before the 1992 convention my working-class supporters wanted to kick the leftists' behinds. When I first laid out the unity tactic, our plan to support whoever got the nomination, their response was, "We're gonna do WHAT?"

The gay contingent wanted to wage a fight and then walk out. And they weren't alone. I told them Peace and Freedom was the only party where we even had a shot at winning and that you fall on your face many times on the road to victory.

We didn't walk out. It was worth it. Afterward, Cathy, a young middle-class white woman, one of our delegates, told me, "I was very naive. I grew up during this convention. I realize that there are 'progressive' people who, if they ever got to run this country, would not include the majority of ordinary people." The convention taught this better than I could have. And there are lots of Cathys out there.

I lost the nomination and still called for unity. Even a Daniels delegate acknowledged, "It's easier to call for unity when you win than when you lose." There was a sense that something powerful had happened at that convention, and I was leading it. There were some people who told me privately that I should have had the nomination but admitted that even though they supported our politics, they just didn't have the guts to stand up and say so. To make these people more powerful, we have to grow.

3

THE DEMOCRATS AND ME

But few were prepared for the next card Jackson had up his sleeve. On March 28, 1971, Jackson quickly moved back onto page one. The Chicago Sun-Times *headlines: "A Black for President among Jesse's Goals." Jackson announced that he was extending his leave from the movement to organize a third party — the Liberation Party — whose membership would be made up of blacks and liberal white elements...Jackson fumed at the thought his announcement was not taken seriously. "A black for president of this country is certainly not a joke. It would give people a choice between two evils, the Republican and Democratic parties — that snake with two heads."*

— *JESSE JACKSON: AMERICA'S DAVID* BY BARBARA REYNOLDS, 1985

People have illusions about Jesse Jackson. I don't think there's any mystery, though: he's the leader of the atrophied left wing of the Democratic Party. He has repeatedly made it clear *by his actions* (not his words) that his loyalty is to the Democratic Party, not to the Black community, not to working people, not to progressives or to labor. Now I think it's up to the people who've supported him to recognize that and to leave him. He left us a long time ago.

Jesse isn't the only Black politician trying to grab something from the current political situation. A lot of Black Democrats know they have no power; they're making self-conscious decisions to go with what's best for *them*, not what's best for their constituencies. Similarly, the women candidates who paraded across the stage at the 1992 Democratic Party convention in New York City were doing what they thought was in their best interests; they weren't concerned with what the women of this country need, or want.

Black Democrats are very protective of one another. It's a club. That's why they never challenge Jesse. I caught him on TV representing the Democratic Party in a debate with John Sununu, the former White House chief of staff, who was representing the Republicans. The debate was about who would be most hurt by a Perot candidacy, the Democrats or the Republicans. Jesse was defending the Democratic Party. What about defending the Black community? What about defending poor people? What about defending the unions? Well, as far as Jesse's concerned, that's not his job.

It was more a test of morality than politics. For more than a week, the Rev. Jesse Jackson flunked. When asked whether he had referred to Jews as "Hymie" and to New York City as "Hymie town," Jackson said over and over, "I have no recollection." But at a Manchester synagogue two days before the New Hampshire primary, Jackson finally admitted making the offensive comments. "In private talks we sometimes let our guard down and become thoughtless," he explained. "It was not in a spirit of meanness, but an off-color remark having no bearing on religion or politics. However innocent and unintended, it was insensitive and wrong."

— *TIME*, MARCH 12, 1984

The relationship between Blacks and Jews, as orchestrated by the Democratic Party, is patronizing. We are building something

very different between Blacks and Jews in the independent political movement. The Jewish activists who work with me aren't
trying to buy the Black community politically. They are giving
their history — the complex history of the Jewish people as victims of the vicious genocide that was the Holocaust — to advance the fight against racism. Jesse's "Hymietown" remark reflected the fact that Blacks and Jews in the Democratic Party
hate each other; the way the party has historically organized that
relationship sparks this kind of antagonism.

Ann Lewis, who was a political consultant to Jesse during
his 1988 campaign, is a case in point. She is a Jewish woman,
and what I call a liberal racist. She's always related to me as if I
were dirt. Gerald Austin, Jesse's campaign manager in 1988, is
another example of a liberal Jewish racist. He began trashing
Jesse the moment that he lost the Democratic nomination in
'88 and Austin was out of a job.

Blacks and Jews in NAP have serious discussions about our
differences — that's an ongoing (and necessary) part of the
process of building the independent political movement together. Contrary to the anti-Semitic and racist (not to mention sex-
ist) way in which our detractors caricature my relationship with
Fred Newman (he is "shrewd" and "manipulative"; I am "naive" and "passive"), I think what we have built together is a
model for Black/Jewish relationships.

The nature and quality of what we've built gets expressed
in how we talk; it explains why I don't use language like "Hymietown" — even in "private talks."

*Mr. Sharpton has surprised a lot of people in this unpredictable
political year.*

— *NEW YORK TIMES,* JULY 28, 1992

I think that Fred is the reason the coalition between NAP and Reverend Sharpton has survived as long as it has. Fred isn't reactive. That isn't to say he doesn't have reactions (like everyone else) — he just doesn't let himself be determined by them. He's not societally arrogant.

I've been on the front lines of NAP's relationship with Rev, as people with whom he is close call him, from Atlantic City to Los Angeles. He's more uptight when we're together in New York City — I think — because the Black nationalists are on his back about working with NAP.

During the New York primary Ramona Whaley, a Black psychologist who was a member of Rev's campaign committee when he was seeking the Democratic Party nomination for the U.S. Senate, got into a conversation with Jessie Fields, a leader of the New Alliance Party who was running for Congress in Harlem against Charles Rangel, the incumbent, at a candidates' forum; Ramona said some nasty things about me to Jessie. I called Ramona up and told her that if she had political differences with me, as an African American sister she should tell me directly. She said she didn't like some of the things I was "into."

"I'm into the Black community," I responded. "What don't you like about the Black community?" She hung up on me.

Ramona belongs to the New York chapter of the Association of Black Psychologists, an organization which has been tremendously unfriendly to me and to NAP. Ramona's irrational about NAP. So are some other Black nationalists. I put political issues on the table but they won't respond. Rev was joking with me about the Peace and Freedom Party convention in California, which was kind of a madhouse, but like a picnic in the country compared to the New York scene. He said, "After the primary, give me an assignment in California — I can handle those leftists in my sleep."

I feel fiercely loyal to Rev because of how badly he is treated by the Black Democrats. During the primary Jesse Jackson came into town to pull out the vote for Rev, Representative Floyd Flake, the Queens congressman, and Representative Ed Towns, the chairman of the Congressional Black Caucus. But Jesse wouldn't say that was what he was doing. He called it "voter registration." This was two days *after* the voter registration deadline. Why? Because he was afraid to support Rev openly. Jesse thinks the Black community is stupid. He and some of his fellow "militants" even went into court to "demand" an extension of the voter registration deadline — after it had already passed. It wasn't serious.

One night shortly before the primary I went to an event in Brooklyn. Jesse spoke first, and then Rev. When Jesse speaks, you feel like he's pulling your strings — saying what Black leaders say to get Black folks to jump up out of their seats. Rev speaks from his history. I was proud of being connected to him.

I'm *used* to everyone — the Black Democrats, the Black nationalists — treating me badly. Jitu Weusi, a member of Sharpton's campaign committee and a longtime NAP foe (though he did endorse my first gubernatorial run) uses Black women to harass me. In 1989, when I was "dogging" David Dinkins (following him all over the city with the demand that he be accountable to the Black and Latino communities which would elect him), I went out to an event in Brooklyn where he was speaking. I walked into the room and everyone went into shock. I wasn't even planning to do anything — I just wanted Dave to know I was there. A Black man came up to me to tell me that two women — one of them turned out to be Jitu's wife — had said that they were going to "kick my ass." He was concerned and he wanted to escort me to my car.

Like Ramona Whaley, another one of his "hit women," Jitu

has never been willing to have a political dialogue with me because he's afraid I'll reveal that he takes his orders from the white controllers of the Democratic Party. When he attacks my relationship with Fred, it's not because Fred's white (which is what Jitu, reading from his Black nationalist script, *says* is the problem); Jitu works with and for white people — he takes white money — all the time. What Jitu doesn't like about Fred is not his skin pigment but his politics.

When I was on the road in '88, the Black nationalists related to me as if I were an assimilationist. I'm not. Nor am I a nationalist. People talk as if there are only two categories. I'm independent; I'm the Black leader of a multi-racial movement, a working-class movement.

Neither nationalism nor assimilationism is going to take the Black community anywhere. It's already been decided that we're *unassimilable* in American society as it is. So the assimilationists are telling the Black community to do something that we can't, which is to become like white people. As for the Black nationalists, when's the last time that Black people got organized to get on a boat to go back to Africa?

BALTIMORE (AP)—An association of black newspaper publishers denounced Democratic presidential candidate Bill Clinton Thursday for backing out of an appearance at its national convention after wanting to be included.

The National Newspaper Publishers Association said Clinton reneged after learning that Lenora Fulani, a fringe candidate who disrupted an April Clinton speech in New York City, would be on the same platform.

During an angry press conference, leaders of the 205-newspaper association said Clinton's staff requested in January that he be allowed to appear, then canceled 48 hours before the event...

Clinton spokeswoman Dee Dee Myers, traveling with the candidate, said that Clinton "would not appear on the same program with Fulani." She said the campaign "tried hard to find an alternate" time to appear at the conference without success.

— ASSOCIATED PRESS, JUNE 11, 1992

Throughout the campaign Clinton put tremendous effort into defining his center-right politics. He's a good talker, and most people aren't informed enough to ask any hard questions. If Bill Clinton had been willing to expose himself politically, he wouldn't have refused to appear on the same stage with me at the National Newspaper Publishers Association forum — but he was afraid to.

Clinton isn't smart enough to maintain his farce on the stage with me (at least he was smart enough to know that!). Besides, if he and I appeared on the stage together, many more people would be exposed to me and my politics. What I was saying, straight up, to Black America, to Latino America, to white America, was that they couldn't let Bill Clinton get away with saying that he'd be "hard on the niggers."

I feel a combination of frustration and fear about moving people en masse. At the NNPA there were people in the audience who were ready to follow me out the door and into the streets! I had gotten them to hear some things that they had no intention of hearing when they walked in.

Clearly, we're on the brink of something — I'm now in a position to make more and more demands on people, and that's something I want and need to do better. Before, I was doing all that I could do. *Sometimes* now I have the experience that I've left no stone unturned, but I'm very aware that there's

a gap between how many people are out there ready to be organized and how many I'm actually organizing.

*Responding to criticism by Gov. Bill Clinton that remarks she
made in a newspaper interview were hate-filled and divisive,
the rap artist Sister Souljah yesterday characterized the
Arkansas Governor as a hypocrite and called his remarks "a
poor excuse for an agenda-less candidate."...*

*The news conference was called to respond to remarks made by
Mr. Clinton on Saturday at a meeting of the Rev. Jesse Jackson's
Rainbow Coalition in Washington. Mr. Clinton chided the
Rainbow Coalition for giving a platform to the rap artist.*

— *NEW YORK TIMES,* JUNE 17, 1992

I was sort of stunned by the cover-up of what happened at the
NNPA meeting — how quickly the news became Sister Souljah.
The media all said that Clinton was being "strong" in attacking
Sister Souljah and Jesse. But for a white male politician to say to
white America, "The Black community doesn't mean anything
to me" isn't a strong statement. It's a racist one. White politicians have been saying that for centuries.

There was something hilarious about the commotion over
Sister Souljah. There I was, a Black woman running for the
presidency of the United States, who was raising fundamental
issues about the deregulation of democracy and about the
Black Agenda, but the media and the other candidates
couldn't bring themselves to mention my name. And there was
Sister Souljah, a rap artist. And the governor of New York
state, Mario Cuomo, was calling on Bill Clinton and Jesse
Jackson to "smoke a peace pipe" and end their fight over her,
as if this had been a high-level political dispute. But they'll talk

about *anything* other than the independent option for the Black community.

Around the time of the Clarence Thomas confirmation hearings, I was pointing out how the liberals — Black and white — loved Anita Hill, the Black woman who accused Thomas of sexual harassment. The liberals were falling all over each other to come to Hill's defense. There I was being viciously attacked, taking all kinds of risks, and none of the liberals would utter a word in my defense.

The Black male leadership of the Democratic Party, who know the difference between Sister Souljah and me, figured out quickly how to use that whole incident with her and Clinton; they could support Black women without rocking the boat. I don't begrudge the support for Sister Souljah. But what are the American people going to get from this? Nothing. Sister Souljah was the nationalists' Anita Hill.

I've been doing independent politics for a long time now. I've led the building of the fourth-largest party in this country. But many people are still trying to keep me invisible. You'd think liberals, for instance, would be knocking down the doors trying to find out what we know. Instead, they act as if we don't exist. Ultimately, though, I think that these omissions don't do us any real harm; they actually illuminate the contradictions of liberalism.

Reading the newspapers gives me the impression that we're invisible. And it feels so invigorating! The powers-that-be are scared of what's really going on in the country. One day the *Amsterdam News,* New York's pre-eminent Black newspaper, wrote pages and pages about independent politics and not one word about NAP. It's as if they think that if they don't mention NAP then we don't exist. But the silence is very loud. Not just our supporters, but reporters, ask me why they don't know about me. People are hungry for independent politics.

I had a conversation with Congressman Rangel about co-sponsoring a debate at the Apollo on where the Black vote should go in 1992. He said that since the primaries were finished, the debates were over. I asked him how that could be, given how *uncommitted* the Black vote was. The next day I opened the newspaper and Rangel was threatening to vote for Perot! It was safer for Black Democrats to go with Ross Perot (for a while) than with us. Perot didn't have very much of a connection to the Black community. He didn't go all-out to galvanize Black support for independent politics. I did, and do — which is why Perot was safer.

In a sharply worded criticism of developments, Jackson's Rainbow Coalition recently issued its own 1992 platform, which declares on the last page: "In the middle of a national economic crisis, we have three conservative candidates running for president," effectively lumping Clinton together with President Bush and Ross Perot.

— *WASHINGTON POST*, JULY 13, 1992

President Bill Clinton. You have survived a tough spring. It will make you stronger for the fall. With your stripes you must heal and make us better. The hopes of many depend upon your quest. Be comforted that you do not stand alone.

— REVEREND JESSE JACKSON, SPEECH BEFORE THE DEMOCRATIC NATIONAL CONVENTION, JULY 14, 1992

I've been marching in the Caribbean Day parade for many years. Labor Day, 1992 was the first time I spoke at the rally that's always held afterward. And it was the first time that Reverend Sharpton marched with the Democrats.

The march started two hours late because Mayor Dinkins and Governor Cuomo were late coming from the Labor Day parade in Manhattan. The Caribbean Chamber of Commerce, which sponsors the event, was having a breakfast. So I went in, hung out, and gave interviews.

I saw Jesse and Rev go into the bank together. This is the bank where we brought Bridgette Amos to confront Mayor Dinkins after her son Tony had been shot by a police officer, just days after Gavin Cato was killed in Crown Heights. It's a place where "dignitaries" can hide from the masses. I went into the bank to get my parade badge. The media were asking Jesse a lot of questions. I mingled, chatted with Ed Towns, the Brooklyn congressman (who despite his worries defeated his machine-backed challenger in the primary two days later), and other folks. Tons of people were there. I walked over and watched Jesse watch me while he was talking to the reporters.

When Jesse saw me coming toward him he finished what he was saying and walked away abruptly. I walked toward him — no one there was willing to stop me. He was unfriendly but not hostile. He did the minimum, to get our brief conversation over with as soon as possible. Rev said hi to me.

I just floated around from person to person. Lorraine Stevens, a founder of NAP who was running for state assembly against Roger Green in Brooklyn's 57th assembly district, Alvaader Frazier, an attorney who is often with me at such events, Yvonne Murray, a Brooklyn community activist who works closely with me, and some other people were all there as part of my "entourage." We sat at the door of the bank waiting for things to start.

During the last weeks of the campaign, as I was being increasingly candid and open on Black radio stations, more and more Black men were coming over to thank me for telling them the truth. A sponsor of the parade told me that I had taught him more politics than anyone else. David Dinkins walked in. I went up to him and said, "Hello, Mr. Mayor" and he said, "Hello, Dr. Fulani."

Then it's Mario Cuomo's turn. Unlike Jesse, Governor Cuomo can afford to speak to me. In fact, he wants to — he's such an egomaniac; he likes to show that he can talk to the radicals. But Alvaader doesn't realize this. So she rushed over to him and spun him around, forcing him to face me, which was unnecessary, since he had already stopped to speak to me!

So we had this *scene:* While Cuomo and I were speaking, and the cameras were snapping, Alvaader was pushing the photographers and reporters back — and Cuomo's security were pushing *her.* As for my dialogue with the governor —

Cuomo: Hi, Dr. Fulani. I haven't seen you around lately. I thought you were running, but I haven't seen you in the debates.

Fulani: That's because your party and the Republican Party are so exclusive and undemocratic that independents aren't allowed in the debates.

Cuomo: You know my position on electoral reform.

Fulani: We have this conversation every time we meet. It doesn't change anything. I know your position better than you do. If you want to do something, do something with Timothy Penny's bill!

I was referring to the Democracy in Presidential Debates Act introduced by the Congressman from Minnesota, which I hoped the Subcommittee on Elections would hold hearings on during the upcoming session.

I think it's kind of funny: what Cuomo was trying to convey was, "I'm so bad I can even talk to Lenora Fulani."

Finally, a million Democrats ran out the door carrying CLINTON/GORE signs and entered the street in a clump.

These big-time Black Democrats — Jesse Jackson, David Dinkins — were at Cuomo's side. Reverend Sharpton was with them. Al Vann, the Brooklyn state assemblyman, and Jitu Weusi, both mainstays of the Black Democratic reform machine in Brooklyn, brought up the rear. Lorraine, Alvaader, Yvonne and I, with the rest of our contingent (about 10 people in all) kept ourselves at a distance of half a block behind them. I pointed at Cuomo, Jackson and Co. and yelled to the crowd, "Those are the Democrats who fucked you over. Vote independent, vote for me!" The people cheered like mad.

We got to the bandstand where the dignitaries sit to listen to the speakers. Someone in the crowd asked me why I wasn't over on the speakers' platform. So I took Lorraine and Yvonne and walked over to the stage. A man told me that I couldn't come up because there were "too many people." In that case, I said, he should tell Liz Holtzman, the Brooklyn district attorney and, like Rev, a candidate for the U.S. Senate, to get off the stage. Suddenly, he decided that there was room for me. All the Democrats were clumped around Jesse on the right side of the stage, which had slumped down in the middle because of the weight. I was on the left. People in the crowd were watching me watch Jesse. It was great. They were winking, and making faces, and gesturing to me in response to what he was saying.

Jesse was cheerleading for David Dinkins, urging "four more years" for the mayor. He attacked Bush and Quayle. He did his voter registration routine. He never mentioned Clinton's name. Then the crowd started yelling for Sharpton. Rev took the mike. I asked when my turn was and was told, "You can talk whenever you want to." As I started to walk across the stage, I looked down at the floor to avoid all the wires and the middle section, which had collapsed. By the time I got to the other side and looked up (which was 20 seconds later), all the Democrats had disappeared!

I told the crowd that neither the Democrats nor the Republicans gave a damn about the Black community, and that Clinton had kicked Jesse in the teeth. Everybody went mad. People were cheering, booing. The whole thing was transformed. Members of the band asked for my autograph. The organizers would never have invited me to speak but, since I was there, they couldn't exclude me.

My message to the Black community was, "Wake up! We tolerate so much abuse. How can we give Clinton even one vote?" Where was the Black community in 1992? Why wouldn't they do for me what white folks did for Perot? The answer is — bad voting habits. The Black leadership plays a crucial role in perpetuating those habits.

During the campaign I was interviewed by the *Final Call*, the newspaper of the Nation of Islam. I told the interviewer that the conventions of the two major parties had nothing to do with the fate of the Black community. The NAP convention had much more do with that fate. Why hadn't we been covered?

Why had Sister Souljah and Bill Clinton been on the paper's front page? How come I wasn't? What statement were the editors making?

What's that all about? The *Final Call* can't support me without catching heat from Democratic Party politicos, which shows how very controversial NAP is. If I invented the cure for racism (or for AIDS), there are certain Black leaders who wouldn't touch it for no other reason than that I had invented it.

NAP's become the litmus test in the electoral movement.

With Ross Perot having validated independent politics, there was no excuse for the Black leadership to ignore my campaign — except for their tenuous hold on the status quo. White America is leaving the Democratic Party in droves. There soon won't be anybody left but the Black community and Bill Clinton. That's a sorry state of affairs!

The only people who can remedy all this is the Black community. Black people *need* politics that can do something about the mess America's in. But the Black community has been persuaded to "want" more nationalist politics, or more Democratic Party politics. There has to be a struggle over which route we're going to go.

I like going out to the Black community and raising these issues. I *want* to have this fight. But most Black elected officials don't even have the guts to have a public dialogue. When I did a radio show a while back, a man in the audience said to me, "If you couldn't hold your marriage together, how can you run the country?" The rest of the audience was furious. But of all the things I may feel vulnerable about, that's not one of them. I knew it was a political attack from someone whose job it was to protect the two-party system. That's how the Democrats fight — nasty.

4

REV. AL SHARPTON, MY PARTNER IN LIBERATION

Yusuf Hawkins, 16 years old, was killed on August 23, 1989 in the Bensonhurst area of Brooklyn by a gang of white men. Reverend Sharpton and I had known each other for four or five years at that point, working together on various cases of racial violence — Bernhard Goetz, the white vigilante who shot four Black youth on a New York City subway train; Michael Griffith, a young Black man chased to his death by a gang of whites in the Howard Beach section of Queens; and Tawana Brawley, a Black teenager from Wappingers Falls, New York whose rape provoked one of the most bitter political/racial battles in recent history.

Rev and I marched together and sat in courtrooms together. He took a considerable amount of heat in becoming identified as the militant spokesperson for the Black poor. I stood with him during all of these struggles and I got to know him well. But it was really after Yusuf was killed that our connection deepened and our influence on each other grew. What had begun as a relationship of mutual support progressed into a political alliance which irritated a lot of people and which has had to endure constant attempts to break it up.

Black Youth Is Killed by Whites; Brooklyn Attack Is Called Racial.

— *NEW YORK TIMES*, AUGUST 25, 1989

I first met Yusuf's parents — Moses Stewart and Diane Hawkins — at the Slave theater on Fulton Street in Brooklyn, where Rev and Alton Maddox, the very brilliant and brash civil rights attorney, led weekly meetings of the United African Movement. I went to the Slave every week for two years, in the heat of all the battles around Yusuf's murder, and I marched with Moses and Diane through the streets of Bensonhurst during the trials of Yusuf's killers.

What typically happens with cases of racial violence that gain public attention is that, for a while, there's a lot of coverage in the media and a lot of activity on the part of different political forces with a stake in the outcome. With Diane and Moses, that attention lasted through the trial. Then, when almost everyone had gotten what they came for, the cameras went away. Moses had been in the limelight. A lot of people had been all over him. Everybody loved him. Then it was finished and he was left standing there — by everyone but us. Rev and I stayed with Moses and Diane long after the "glamour" of the tragedy was gone. I deeply respected Moses and Diane for standing up to those who had been responsible for the vicious murder of their son. Rev, Fred Newman and I gave them whatever support we could to help them sustain that fight. It was very moving to me that this family could turn to our political community. More than just giving them things, we helped them to create and build something.

Moses and Diane, Rev and I were all in the movement together. Moses went to Reverend Sharpton for some things, and he came to me — and eventually to Fred — for other things.

It was in this context that my relationship to Rev developed, that the movement grew and advanced.

That "politics makes strange bedfellows" is clearly tangible in lower Manhattan, where a collective of radical artists has set up an arts center...[The Castillo Cultural Center] includes a photo lab, a theater, a gallery, the publishing house, an architectural workshop and a construction shop.

— NEW YORK *DAILY NEWS,* NOVEMBER 1, 1989

For a period of about a year, Moses was employed by Castillo International, the Castillo Cultural Center's commercial publishing and recording arm. He was a spokesperson for Castillo books, tapes and records — some of which were products of the coalition between the New Alliance Party and Reverend Sharpton. Castillo International had produced a video called *Yusuf's Movement,* a documentary of the two-year fight for justice for Yusuf's family, which was premiered at an event sponsored by the Yusuf Hawkins Memorial Fund, and held at the Castillo Center in lower Manhattan to commemorate the second anniversary of his death. At my request, Mayor David Dinkins declared the day of the event to be Yusuf Hawkins Day, and issued a proclamation that was presented at the commemoration. Spike Lee, whose film *Jungle Fever* was dedicated to Yusuf, gave permission for some footage from the movie to be used as part of the documentary. I organized young graffiti artists to paint a mural dedicated to Yusuf on a wall off Fulton Street in Brooklyn (the wall was donated by a local store owner). Moses traveled to different parts of the country and gave presentations on the products and his experiences as Yusuf's father.

We used that video to teach people to move beyond grieving, or chalking up Yusuf's death to another "inevitable" murder of yet another Black youth who was in the wrong place at the wrong time. We wanted to create an organized response to racial violence, which includes taking it into the voting booth.

Building that movement was the basis of my relationship with Moses and Diane, which was very powerful, and strong. While Moses worked at Castillo, Diane worked for the Yusuf Hawkins Memorial Fund, which had been set up by Gabrielle Kurlander, the head of Castillo International. The people at Castillo helped Moses to get an apartment (he and Diane had split up by then), set it up, and stabilize himself. But that didn't work out, in part because various Black politicos — who really couldn't have cared less about what happened to Moses — were whispering to him that the work he was doing for Castillo was demeaning. During the build-up for the commemoration event, for example, Moses asked Percy Sutton, the owner of Inner City Broadcasting — the parent company of WLIB and WBLS, the two leading Black radio stations in New York — to contribute to the Fund. Sutton refused, saying he only wanted to give money to Moses personally. I was glad, anyway, that the pressure of the commemoration forced some folks to give Moses and Diane *something.*

Moses and Diane got a lot of flak about the memorial from Bill Tatum, the publisher of the *Amsterdam News,* and other folks who didn't want to give NAP or me any credit for doing for Moses and Diane what everybody should have been doing. Meanwhile, nobody was saying any of this to my face. The same people who were conducting a whispering campaign against me would smile and embrace me when I walked into a room. But I always felt that it all really had more to do with their nastiness toward Moses. Even though Spike Lee dedicated *Jungle Fever* to Yusuf, Spike didn't even introduce Moses and Diane at the opening of the movie; it was that level of rip-off.

I don't think I'll ever really know how much pressure Moses

was under — I'm sure a lot, and I'm sure from some people who wouldn't give him the right time of day. I know he got white-baited, Jew-baited and red-baited. Sometimes he would talk about it.

For most families whose child has been killed, once the case comes to an end legally, all they're left with is their grief and the little bit of justice that they may have been given, if any. These working-class families are beset by all the struggles that they were going through before the murder: they don't get along; there are family hostilities and rivalries; people drink and do drugs. When you get involved with them, you get involved in everything that's going on in their lives. If you don't have something to organize them into, to do something productive, your relationship with them "naturally" peters out.

We were attempting to provide Moses and Diane with another option, by giving them the opportunity to help build a memorial to Yusuf — Moses had asked us to do that. It was clear that there were a lot of people who would support it. And there was a tremendous need to raise money to rent buses to take people to demonstrations and rallies, to become involved in similar cases around the country. The Yusuf Hawkins Memorial Fund was a vehicle to raise money for these cases, to broaden what had happened in Bensonhurst, and at the same time to give Diane a job.

Moses was very responsive and giving to Fred Newman, the executive director of Castillo — he was very aware that Fred had marched with him and had been generous to him — and he gave credit where credit was due: Moses would get up on a stage at a public meeting and acknowledge Reverend Sharpton, Fred and me. Moses and I were friends. I was someone he respected, and I think loved. I loved him also. I think he built the strongest relationship with Fred. Moses understood and appreciated that Fred was there for him and his family, and that Fred was willing to invest in him — not just by giving him money, but by giving him a shot.

We were demanding that Moses and Diane do something with their grief that would allow them to grow. As awful as this might sound, there's a way in which people in their situation get spoiled; other people don't put demands on you so much as they cater to you. Then one day it's over. We weren't interested in having that kind of tokenistic relationship to either of them. We wanted to create the possibility for them to do some growing beyond what their lives had been — to use what had happened to give something back to the community, and also to get some stuff for themselves in a way that was more grown up.

Moses and Diane were thrust into a situation that was extremely challenging, personally and politically; suddenly they found themselves in the midst of a whirlwind and it was very painful and very hard. These ordinary working-class people were living their lives, and then this tragedy struck: their son got off at the wrong subway stop and they were in the middle of one of the most outrageous racial murders in the history of this city, indeed of America. It made national headlines. They were on the front page. They were under attack for having chosen the "wrong" allies to fight their battle. At various times they had thousands of people around the country supporting them. They went through the horrendous experience of the trials, and of knowing that most of their child's murderers never even came to trial, let alone paid for what they had done. Along with Reverend Sharpton, we worked to turn all of this into a more historic fight so that we were strengthened in the ongoing battle against racial injustice. Through all these ups and downs, Rev and Fred and I grew much closer.

I think Rev respected what we were willing and able to do

for Moses and Diane. Rev and I both learned how much being loyal to our people meant to both of us. That is a bond we have. Fred still supports Moses and Diane financially, but I think everyone feels badly that Moses and Diane couldn't sustain their political involvement. Even so, they inspired many, many people to go on — including me.

By the 1960s...Jews had displaced the Irish as the city's policers and tutors of the unwashed; they would be to the blacks and Puerto Ricans what the Irish had been to them and the WASPs to the Irish. It cannot be surprising, then, that, to a southern black plunged suddenly into myriad encounters with Jews who decided whether he could get credit, welfare, an apartment, a job, a passing grade in school, or an acquittal in court, everyone in authority seemed Jewish.

— THE CLOSEST OF STRANGERS: LIBERALISM AND THE POLITICS OF RACE IN NEW YORK, BY JIM SLEEPER, 1990

Fred and Rev did their first forum on Blacks and Jews in January of 1990; that year Rev began inviting NAP to participate in his marches, and our coalition came into existence. We did almost everything together over the next year, up to and including dealing with the assassination attempt against him.

Reverend Sharpton was stabbed on January 12, 1991. Hundreds of people from all over the country were in New York City that weekend to attend a meeting of NAP's national organizers, and we brought 10 busloads to march with Rev in Bensonhurst that Saturday to protest the acquittal of Joey Fama, one of the whites who participated in Yusuf's murder. I was thrilled to be able to give that to our organizers and Rev.

It was a cold day. Rev, Fred and I had all driven out with security teams in our cars. The buses were all parked on the street and the police had us drive our three cars into the schoolyard of P.S. 205 on 20th Avenue. There were 300 cops on hand. Because it was so cold and because we were waiting for everyone to get off the buses and line up, we all sat waiting in our cars. Then, when the schoolyard filled up and it looked like it was time to get started, Fred, Rev and I got out of our cars. Moses was there. So were Jennifer Joseph, Rev's aide, and the Reverend Wayne Stokeling, a close colleague of Rev's.

We were all standing around, sizing up the crowd and waiting for Rev to choose the moment to start, when the stabbing went down. I wasn't very far from Rev, so I saw everything that happened — in a blur. First I was aware of a commotion, and then I saw this guy (he was later identified as Michael Riccardi, the son of a former city transit police officer) run up to Rev. I saw Rev drop to his knees, the knife sticking out of his chest, and I realized what had happened. I was about to step over to him when I saw that Fred and Jennifer were already there, and I knew that they were going to take care of Rev. Meantime, Moses took off after Riccardi with a vengeance. The cops were just standing there — not doing anything. They had let Riccardi through the police lines and it looked as if they were about to let him escape. Moses jumped on Riccardi and then the cops jumped on Moses. Everyone was yelling. I yelled for Jessie Fields, a physician, and she rushed right over to Rev, who was clutching his chest and trying to breathe. I had told the cops to call an ambulance. They had a dozen cars and a mobile command center on site, but they couldn't manage to get an ambulance there. Fred decided we couldn't wait anymore and Dr. Fields and Jennifer agreed, so they decided to take Rev to the hospital in my car. They put Rev in the back seat with Jessie (one of the few cops on the scene who had any presence of mind jumped in with them); Fred sat in the front next to my driver and the car sped out of the schoolyard to Coney Island Hospital. Fred later told me that he and Jessie kept talking to Rev the whole way to the hospital to keep him conscious.

The big issue then was what the demonstrators were going to do. Naturally, people were extremely upset and everyone was running around. It was a strange combination of bedlam and everything being crystal clear: the demonstrators had to be given direction. I decided that I needed to take control of the situation, so I got up on a car and told people that they had to cool out: I said that Rev was hurt, he was on his way to the hospital, he was with a doctor and we would know in time what was going on. Meanwhile, I said, we couldn't afford to have a riot out there in the schoolyard with these cops just waiting for something to jump off so they could start shooting. I was very strong in that, because the cops didn't seem particularly friendly and I still didn't know how the hell Riccardi had been allowed to pass through 300 police officers.

I took charge because we were responsible for all those people who were there. I have a lot of training in being responsible for crowds, in part because I've done so many marches with Reverend Sharpton. Rev and I have gone through some heavy stuff together. When he was locked up with leaders of the Forgotten Youth during a march in Atlantic City, I was outside with the kids — who were very, very, angry — doing crowd control.

I knew I couldn't give in to all the different things I was feeling, because that would have meant that there was no leadership out there. I was scared that Rev was going to die, and at the same time I was aware that if there was anyone people were going to listen to — with Rev gone — it was me. I figured all that out fast, got up on a car, and told people that we were going to march and that they had to do what I was telling them to do. I think that, otherwise, many, many people would have gotten hurt. The cops were just waiting for people to lose it.

Many of the men who were with us from the United African Movement, who in previous marches had been pretty unfriendly to NAP's multi-racial contingents and to me, asked me what I wanted them to do and where I wanted them to go. These brothers were following my leadership. It was very moving. Together with Michael Hardy and some other folks, they got the march going.

The cops came over and asked me if I wanted them to protect me. I told them to get out of my face. Obviously, if the kind of security they were capable of with 300 of them standing around had led to Reverend Sharpton being stabbed, I didn't need them. Some of the marchers stepped forward to do security, including Tony Rose, a very successful African American music producer who works with Castillo International (he was associated with Maurice Starr, the producer whiz behind New Kids on the Block). They were fierce and so was I. That was probably the hardest march I've ever done in my life.

We were out there for about an hour, marching. Kids were chanting, and the tension was so heavy you could smell it. I led people to the church where a few weeks earlier Rev and I had met with some of the white elected officials and community and religious leaders in Bensonhurst. We stood there for a moment of silence, and then headed back to the schoolyard. On our way I got a message that Rev was okay, that he wasn't going to die. I announced the news to the crowd, and told people to get on their buses. I made sure everyone got out of the neighborhood. The NAP folks went back to the convention.

Then I went to the hospital. It was very emotional and very scary. Fred had his staff reach Kathy Jordan, Rev's wife, at work the minute they got to the hospital. Fred was worried that Kathy would hear about the stabbing on the radio, so he insisted that she be found. She had headed out to the hospital as soon as she got word, so she was there by the time I arrived. David Dinkins was there too, and I confronted him: I wanted to know what he was going to do about what had happened. (Dinkins' people didn't want me to get near him, but I did anyway.) Meanwhile, Fred's staff people started fielding calls from the press — we kept them up to date from the hospital — and also called key people around the country to alert them. We got a message through to Jesse Jackson at the Rainbow Coalition office in Washington, DC and Jesse called back in minutes, very upset. He flew to New York the next morning to visit Rev in the hospital. We also reached Congressman Gus Savage in Illinois.

Fred and I went upstairs to the floor that Rev was on, and he asked to see us. When we went into his room he looked terrible. But he knew exactly what had to happen — he's a brilliant tactician. He told us it was very important that we go back to Bensonhurst the next day and asked us to organize a march. Of course we said we would. And we did.

After the attempt on his life in Bensonhurst, Rev left the Slave, where he and Alton had been holding meetings of the United African Movement. He started holding weekly meetings of the National Action Network up in Harlem. Though the audiences in Harlem were still African American, Rev was broadening his social vision. He was beginning to see that people other than Blacks would support him.

When Rev came to Harlem, he was nervous — he didn't know if anyone would come out to hear him. But it didn't take long for the crowd to build. For the first few months that he was in Harlem, I sat up on the stage. Then, one Saturday, Rev decided he didn't want me up there. He didn't say anything. He didn't have to. I came in one day and Jennifer Joseph escorted me to a seat in the audience. I think a lot of people were pressuring Rev then about our relationship. He wasn't that close with Alton at that time and I think some folks were warning him not to end up too close to me.

I have my own organization, so I didn't need to take over Rev's. My feeling was that whenever he wanted me, I'd be there. I would never hold a rally and *not* invite Reverend Sharpton to sit on the stage. But as an African American woman leader, I do all kinds of things that Black men leaders don't do.

Maddox had stayed at the Slave after Rev left and continued to build the UAM. Rev was doing less with Alton, but nobody talked publicly about what this meant or how anyone — including the two of them — felt about it. At the time of Crown Heights, Alton was already back on the scene; he and Rev reignited their political partnership there.

Blacks, Jews and cops battle in the streets: BROOKLYN RACE RIOT

— *NEW YORK POST,* AUGUST 20, 1991

I had gone out to St. John's University in Queens, New York to participate in a demonstration by students who were protesting the acquittal of four young white men charged with raping a Black student. I was on my way back to Manhattan when I heard that Gavin Cato, a seven-year-old Black child, had been struck and killed in the Crown Heights section of Brooklyn by a car that was part of the motorcade belonging to the Grand Rebbe of the Hasidic Jewish sect known as the Lubavitchers. So

I had my driver go directly to Crown Heights, a predominantly Black community with a politically powerful minority of orthodox Jews. There were hundreds of people in the streets, and media all over the place. I started asking people what had happened. Alton Maddox and Rev — I think they came together — arrived and went into the Catos' house. Up until that point Rev and I had talked every day — either he would call me early in the morning, when he got up, or I would call him. We were doing a lot of political work together, so we consulted with one another frequently. But for the duration of this situation in Crown Heights, we barely spoke.

It was like a war zone out there. I called my Manhattan office to get more security, because I realized that I couldn't leave — the youth were out in the streets and the cops were itching for a fight.

Rev, Alton, Rev. Daughtry and Sonny Carson — after having gone to the precinct to present a set of demands on behalf of the Black community — marched back to the street where Gavin had lived. The Hasidim started throwing rocks, and everyone scattered. I was extremely concerned — it seemed as if there were more cops out there than I had thought there were in the world. At about six or seven in the evening, the male leaders went back into the Catos' house. Meanwhile, 400 or 500 kids — mostly young men in their teens and early twenties — were out on the streets. Their anger was primarily directed not at Jews, but at the police, who were all in riot gear — waiting. I realized that there would be a bloodbath unless someone stopped it. I was shocked that Rev, Alton and Carson had gone into the house because someone had to provide leadership in the streets. I didn't know what to do. I couldn't speak to Rev. So I went to the house next door to the Catos, and asked an elderly lady to let me use her phone. I called Fred and told him that there was no leadership out there. Fred told me to ask the Black women to go into the crowd with me and speak to the young men. I did that, but the women said NO. So I took my aides, JoAnne Sullivan, who is Black, and Lou Hinman, who is white, and we went back outside.

I said, "I know this isn't the most popular position, but I don't care about that. I know you're into being macho. But I can't just walk away. You can't let the cops provoke you. I'm not going to lead you into a bloodbath."

"Who's this Black bitch?" someone yelled.

"You can't talk to her like that. She's Dr. Fulani."

"I don't care who she is!"

We argued from about 7 p.m. until midnight, in the middle of the street, with bottles flying and police sharpshooters on the roof. The kids were ready for a suicide mission, and I was talking some combination of a Black mother's common sense and independent politics! I was saying to them, "Don't get yourselves killed. Why don't you build something with me, so that you're not just reacting to the cops every time something like this goes down?" They were furious, and they were taking their anger out on me. But bit by bit, they started listening.

Meanwhile, every 10 minutes a group would throw bottles, or bricks, at the cops, and the cops would move in on them. This was madness. There was no place to run. I went over to the commanding officer and told him, "We don't need you. You should call David Dinkins and tell him to pull the cops out."

At some point Rev came out of the Catos' house, the crowd cheered, and then he went back in. Afterward Anthony Charles, one of Rev's assistants, told me that Rev said he always knew I was crazy but when he looked out the window and saw me in the middle of the crowd he thought I had lost my mind. Well, you can't have a rational dialogue in those circumstances, but you also can't leave the streets. I built lasting relationships with some of the young men who were there that night.

We finally left at 12:30. When I got home and turned on the TV they were talking about the coup against Mikhail Gorbachev in the Soviet Union. Except for the tanks, the scene in the streets looked just like Crown Heights — the helicopters overhead, the streets all lit up, the cops everywhere.

Gavin was killed on Monday evening. On Tuesday the streets were still very tense, with provocateurs on all sides. I wanted to make a militant statement that would, on the one hand, express the Black community's outrage over Gavin's death, and at the same time assert the community's control over itself and its insistence that it would not be provoked into a senseless outburst which would end up with a violent police action against us. I decided that the way to do that was to lead a march of Black women through Crown Heights on Friday evening — the mothers, wives, sisters and daughters of the Black men whom the cops were longing to shoot. I thought that if it was women marching, people wouldn't get their heads blown off. And I thought it was important for the women to back up the youth.

As soon as I put out the word, though, Rev called and asked me not to do the march. He, Alton and Carson were planning to do one the next day, and he was concerned about diffusing the focus. He was very embroiled in what was a fierce leadership struggle among the Black male leaders, and I think he felt that my leading a march the day before theirs would throw a monkey wrench into his plans.

I voiced my concerns about his march, because it seemed that things could get out of hand. Rev was open. He said he was under a lot of pressure — there were all kinds of fights going on among the male leadership (I wasn't privy to them) and things were very tense. I ultimately agreed to his request.

Rev gave a brilliant and passionate talk at Gavin's funeral, which took place a week after he was killed.

Probers yesterday acknowledged "conflicting stories" in the death of a young East Flatbush, Brooklyn, man felled by police bullets Sunday night, and community activists demanded the indictments of the two officers involved. "The police account of what happened has changed at least twice," Lenora Fulani, of the New Alliance Party, said yesterday. She produced a man who said he witnessed the death of Andel Anthony Amos — and that Amos was shot in the back.

— NEW YORK *DAILY NEWS*, AUGUST 29, 1991

Tony Amos, a 19-year-old Black man, was killed by the cops on Sunday night, in neighboring Flatbush, less than a week after Gavin was killed. Within minutes of the shooting, I got calls from several of the young men I had met in the streets in Crown Heights, to tell me what had happened. When I went out there the next morning, the kids were in the streets and the cops had occupied East Flatbush. I met Tony's mother and father, and I stayed out in the streets with the kids because it was clear that the cops were waiting to move in on them. I put myself between the cops and the youth. All those kids wanted to do was grieve. I told the commanding officer, "What you're doing is provocative, either deliberately or stupidly."

I led a protest march to the 70th police precinct and back. I stopped women along Utica Avenue who were shopping — old women, and young ones with baby strollers — and told them,

"The cops are killing our kids. If we march with them, we'll stop the kids from being killed." There were a lot of women, and a lot of Black youth. I stayed out in Flatbush until we buried Tony. And I persuaded Mayor Dinkins' office to pay for his funeral.

With the exception of a paragraph in an article in *New York Newsday,* the media chose not to cover my presence, and the role that I played, in Crown Heights. They pretended that I didn't exist, as if none of this had gone down.

Today the Hasidic parts of Crown Heights are locked into a sullen ceasefire. The Lubavitchers are observing the High Holy Day season. The New York City Police Department is saturating the streets with cops. And the Caribbean-Americans and African-Americans who share Crown Heights with the Hasidim quietly curse the "occupation army" in their midst. The bloodshed has stopped, but the anger continues — and the tenuous civility that allowed for an uneasy co-existence has yet to be mended.

— *NEW YORK NEWSDAY,* SEPTEMBER 15, 1991

The first Blacks and Jews forum NAP did in Brooklyn in January of 1990, where Rev and Fred were the keynote speakers, established a relationship among Rev, Fred and me. We started meeting to talk about different things, particularly about building a coalitional relationship. The first thing Rev and I did together after that was a press conference on the steps of City Hall. Rev was late. People wanted to start without him. When he arrived we got into a fight. He started yelling at me — in public. I thought he was out of his mind, since *he* was the one who was late! Then I panicked. I thought I had damaged this brand new coalitional relationship.

When I talked to Fred about it, he said that a coalition wasn't about a personality-to-personality relationship, and that we'd probably have many fights — this coalition wasn't going to dissolve because of one fight on the steps of City Hall. Fred pointed out that Rev and I are both very willful. The issue was to figure out how to work together so neither of us felt compromised.

I came to learn that Rev gets extremely tense, extremely anxious, right before an event. It's important to get along with him at that moment. I worked hard to learn who he was. I talked to him on the phone after that press conference and told him that he couldn't yell at me in public. He heard that.

Another time, during my 1990 run for governor of New York — this was the campaign for youth and democracy — State Senator David Paterson, who was supporting Mario Cuomo, held a voter registration rally at the Harlem State Office Building. Rev had been invited to speak, I hadn't. Rev was going to do what he could to get me up there on the stage — to open the way for me. At one point he signaled to me to come up, but I blew the moment and he was left up there alone. To make matters worse, I had an attitude — why is it *you* who's on the stage and not me? I had left him up there holding the bag when he was trying to do something for me. I called him up afterward to apologize. He was lovely.

The lesson I learned from that was the importance of getting up on the stage — you can't just walk away from something because people are treating you badly. I have to go even when it's hard for me to be there. Rev is much better than I am at getting on stages. My attitude is, "The hell with you! I'll stay down here with the people." But that doesn't help anyone.

ATLANTIC CITY, N.J. (AP)—The Rev. Al Sharpton says he plans a Boardwalk protest the day of the Miss America Pageant final to highlight the poverty of the Black community here.

— Associated Press, September 5, 1990

Rev is brilliant at going into a place, or a situation, where everybody says, "You're an outsider" and becoming an insider. Atlantic City was an example. We worked very hard so we could do a march on Labor Day, 1990 in Atlantic City. NAP brought busloads of people down to support the Forgotten Youth, an organization of Atlantic City's African American young people who live in poverty right under the shadow of the city's boardwalk and casinos.

Then in the middle of our demonstration Rev got arrested, and I was left on the streets with a thousand Black youth I didn't know and who didn't know me! They wanted to rush the police station. Adults from the community couldn't control them. I got up on a car with a bullhorn and told them that Rev had asked me to organize a rally, not a riot, and that if anybody was telling them to rush the cops then they could bet those folks were provocateurs. When Rev finally got out of jail I told him that next time I'd go to jail and he could be out on the streets!

Our coalition is based on a successful formula — his popularity and our organization — for building a relationship between a mass leader and the left. I've learned and grown tremendously from the relationship. Fred and Rev both know things about people and politics that I don't. If I hadn't stretched, I would have been in the background. Now, I can go into any community in the country and organize.

Rev is probably one of the few people who works as hard as NAP does. That's why we work well together. He eats, sleeps,

breathes civil rights. He grew up right smack dab in the middle
of mainstream Black political, religious and cultural life. He has
a relationship with virtually every Black political figure, every
preacher, every entertainer in this country. Rev and I have a
partnership based on the liberation of our people. It means a
great deal to me!

At a rally in Manchester, New Hampshire to support deposed Haitian President Jean-Bertrand Aristide. February 1992.

Outside Berlin, New Hampshire in January 1992. With me from left: journalist Phyllis Goldberg, aides JoAnne Sullivan and Lou Hinman, and campaign organizers Jeffrey Aron and Bob Levy.

With my running mate Maria Elizabeth Muñoz after we were unanimously nominated to head up the New Alliance Party's 1992 presidential slate. ▶

With my campaign manager Dr. Fred Newman at the 1992 New Alliance Party presidential nominating convention.

▲ Gauging the sentiment at the grassroots in New Hampshire before throwing my hat into the ring in the nation's first Democratic Party primary. December 1991.

The threat of my leading another massive democracy picket got Larry Agran (center) into the Democratic Party debate in Buffalo, New York in April 1992. At right is my special assistant, Dr. Rafael Mendez. ▼

Campaigning at a paper mill outside Berlin, New Hampshire. January 1992. ▶

Democracy picket outside Lehman College in the Bronx, New York. March 31, 1992. ▼

▲
Leading 300 demonstrators in a protest at Lehman College in the Bronx against the exclusion of insurgent Democrats Eugene McCarthy and Larry Agran from Democratic Party debates. March 31, 1992.

◄ With Debra Olson, Ross Perot's liaison to the lesbian and gay community. September 1992.

With former Senator Eugene McCarthy during the Democratic Party primary in New York. April 2, 1992. ▼

*With Alton Maddox,
Reverend Sharpton and
Yusuf Hawkins' father,
Moses Stewart, during one
of the 33 marches in
Bensonhurst, Brooklyn.
1990.* ▶

*Walking through Harlem
with Moses Stewart and
Reverend Sharpton at the
1990 African American
Day Parade.*
▼

Driving Bill Clinton from Harlem Hospital. March 27, 1992.

Giving the lowdown on the Nation's *front-page attack* at my weekly meeting in Harlem. April 23, 1992.

Before my debate with Ron Daniels at the Apollo theater in Harlem. At center is WLIB talk show host Gary Byrd. 1992.

A little-known New Yorker, Lenora Fulani, bags Fed financing for '92 prez race

THE 624G LONGSHOT

STORY ON PAGE 2

In December of 1991, soon after I qualified for federal primary matching funds, the Daily News, *one of New York's leading dailies, put this "home town girl makes good" headline on the front page.*

I first met the Reverend Jesse Jackson when he spoke at the Black and Puerto Rican Legislative Caucus weekend in Albany, NY in February 1987.

With David Dinkins at a candidates forum held by the Institute for Puerto Rican Policy during New York City's mayoral race in the summer of 1989.

In June 1992 Bill Clinton refused to share a stage with me at the National Newspaper Publishers Association convention, earning him a stinging denunciation from the organization, which represents 30 million Black readers.

▲
Nation of Islam leader
Minister Louis Farrakhan
(standing at rostrum) and
Reverend Sharpton at the
press conference where they
endorsed my 1990 inde-
pendent campaign for gov-
ernor of New York state.
October 17, 1990.

With John Atkisson of Ross
Perot's United We Stand,
America at NAP's presiden-
tial nominating convention.
August 23, 1992.

With members of the
Hempstead, New York
NAACP. Local president
Barbara Powell is standing
third from left. 1992.

Crown Heights, Brooklyn. August 1991.

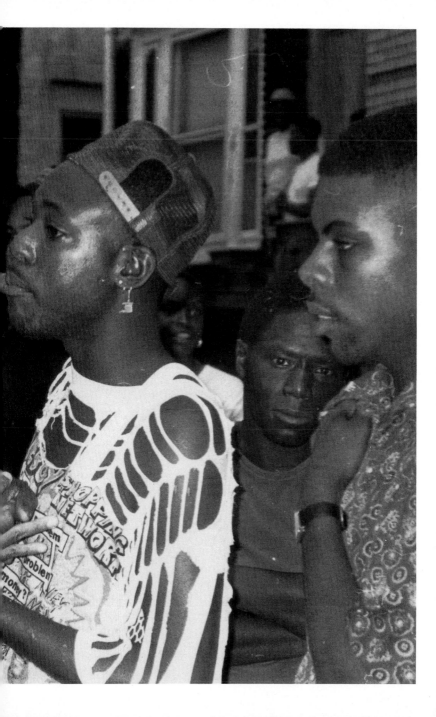

"Doggin' Dinkins" in 1989.

5

BLACK LAWYER PAR EXCELLENCE

Cuomo's appointment of a special prosecutor for Howard Beach, Charles (Joe) Hynes, had been a kind of defeat. He opposed the appointment of special prosecutors generally. He had appointed one in this case only under inflammatory pressure by the black lawyers Alton H. Maddox, Jr., and C. Vernon Mason, and the Reverend Al Sharpton, and by the decision of the black victims to withhold their cooperation, so that the Queens prosecutor could not complete an investigation. With national attention focused on Howard Beach, the state — and Cuomo as its leader — had for a time seemed impotent, unable to resolve the worst case of racism in years.

— *OUTRAGE: THE STORY BEHIND THE TAWANA BRAWLEY HOAX,*
BY A TEAM OF *NEW YORK TIMES* REPORTERS, 1990

"If," I warned the group, "Maddox and Mason want to participate in the questioning, and they probably will, I want everyone to remain cool. They are both criminal lawyers, after all, and they may be of some help. Besides, if we don't win their confidence today, it's all over."

— *INCIDENT AT HOWARD BEACH: THE CASE FOR MURDER,*
BY BROOKLYN DISTRICT ATTORNEY
CHARLES "JOE" HYNES, 1990

Alton Maddox, a well known activist attorney, has been a close colleague of Reverend Sharpton for many years. Alton, a Black nationalist leader based in Brooklyn, and I first met in 1986, when we were protesting the murder of Michael Griffith, a young Black man who was chased into oncoming traffic by a gang of white youths in the Howard Beach section of Queens. I came to know him gradually, as we kept turning up at the same political events. I went to all the rallies and demonstrations to support Tawana Brawley; Alton was working on that case with Rev. I also attended most of the marches in Bensonhurst protesting Yusuf Hawkins' murder; Alton marched in many of them. Alton might have preferred it if NAP weren't at the marches we led together, but I can't remember him ever being overtly hostile toward me; we just have different politics.

I like Alton. I've never been as close to him as I've been to Rev. But my relationship to Alton is straightforward. I find his history — growing up poor in the South, later becoming an activist attorney — very moving and very painful. I think he's been screwed over a lot. In some ways I think that's made him bitter.

I started going to weekly rallies of the United African Movement at the Slave in the Bedford-Stuyvesant neighborhood of Brooklyn every week. They were organized by Rev and Alton.

In October of 1990 Alton, Rev and I did a speaking engagement together on the campus of the State University of New York in Brockport (which is between Buffalo and Rochester). It was during this trip that Alton and I had an extended dialogue about the 1990 gubernatorial race, which Joe Mack, a member of the UAM — who was, in my opinion, trying to keep NAP from getting the 50,000 votes in New York state necessary for a permanent place on the New York ballot — had entered, claiming to be the UAM's candidate. Alton told me that the UAM had not given Mack the go-ahead to run. Mack's campaign caused a big fight within the UAM, which at the time many journalists were asking me about. I always said it was none of their business, since I felt the press was only trying to escalate these tensions.

I was relieved when Rev, Alton and I stopped doing the speaking tour together. We had political differences that made the joint speaking engagements difficult. Alton often made homophobic statements which I didn't like. It was an uncomfortable situation. Rev and I had differences too, but at least he didn't use the word "faggot."

Alton is consistently anti-Jesse Jackson. Once Alton advised that when Jesse came to speak people should stand up and turn their backs on him! Jesse flew in to New York City to see Rev the morning after Rev was stabbed. Alton was very upset — I think partly because Alton hadn't been there with us in Bensonhurst when the stabbing occurred. Alton was also furious at David Dinkins for going on the radio after Rev was stabbed and saying that Rev was calling for calm. Alton's posture was, "The hell with calm! Black people should turn the city inside out!" I had the impression that he and Rev disagreed about what kind of political statement to make after the stabbing, but I wasn't in on their discussions.

Alton and I marched together twice after the stabbing; we didn't see each other much after that. I stopped going to the Slave when Rev moved his weekly meeting to Harlem. There may have been differences between Alton and Rev about me and NAP, but Alton and I were never unfriendly.

Soon after Ron Daniels, the Black leftist who ran for president in nine states, and I debated at the Apollo in Harlem, Alton and I had a brief conversation about Daniels. Even though I had kicked Daniels' ass, he wanted Daniels and me to get together. I said I wasn't interested and that Alton needed to tell Daniels to stop attacking me.

I am today filing disciplinary charges with the grievance committees for Brooklyn, where Mr. Maddox practices, and for Manhattan, where Mr. Mason practices. Specifically, I believe Mr. Maddox and Mr. Mason have violated at least four Disciplinary Rules which govern the conduct of lawyers in New York State...The efforts of Mr. Maddox and Mr. Mason to prevent the truth from coming out failed, as demonstrated by the thorough investigation conducted and the Grand Jury report released today. However, I do not believe that grievance committees should overlook the conduct of these attorneys, the injury their tactics have caused to innocent persons, or the time and expense they have cost the public authorities involved in investigating their spurious charges. Accordingly, I am urging that the grievance committees investigate my charges and take appropriate disciplinary action.

— FROM THE STATEMENT OF NEW YORK STATE ATTORNEY GENERAL ROBERT ABRAMS ANNOUNCING THE FINDINGS OF THE GRAND JURY IN THE TAWANA BRAWLEY CASE, OCTOBER 6, 1988

Prominent activist lawyer Alton Maddox' possible suspension from the bar today for his actions in the Tawana Brawley case would throw three major cases into upheaval. A lawyers' disciplinary committee has requested that Maddox furnish it with any files, documents or other materials related to allegations of professional misconduct lodged against him last year in connection with his handling of the Brawley case.

— *NEW YORK NEWSDAY*, MARCH 12, 1990

After weeks of my trying to reach Alton, and his not returning my calls, I heard from him in another way. He called in to WWRL, New York City's leading gospel radio station, one day during the 1992 presidential campaign while I was on the air. I had just pointed out that other Black leaders have received much more money from Fred Newman than I have, but no one ever attacks *them* as they attack me for my association with Fred.

Alton himself received financial support from Fred when his license to practice law was suspended at the instigation of the attorney general of New York, Robert Abrams, for having accused law enforcement officials and Abrams' office of being involved in a wide-ranging cover-up of the rape of Tawana Brawley, who was being represented by Alton and C. Vernon Mason. Actually, I think Abrams and Governor Mario Cuomo — who had national political ambitions — wanted to punish both Alton and Rev for their role in the Howard Beach case. By insisting that there had to be a special prosecutor to try Michael Griffith's murderers, they were exposing the fact that Black people could not get justice in New York's courts. After Alton was disbarred, no one would come to his defense: not his fellow lawyers, and not Black Democratic Party leaders — who all kept their hands firmly in their pockets. It was Fred Newman who raised $10,000 to support Alton.

After I spoke about this on the radio, Alton called in to the station and said that whatever money we gave him went to defray expenses incurred in connection with Rev's trial. (Abrams brought 67 counts of fraud against Reverend Sharpton, also in retaliation for Howard Beach; Alton did a wonderful job as Rev's lawyer, and a jury acquitted Rev of every charge.) I told Alton, on the air, "We gave you the money. You were free to do whatever you wanted with it. I'm addressing the double standard that's at work here." We had a feisty but decent conversation. It was kind of fun.

Afterward I called him at home. I said that I was angry at him for not responding when Ron Daniels came into New York City and trashed me for my "cult" relationship to Fred. I pointed out that when he, or Rev, or any other Black leader has been attacked, I've come to their defense — often when no one else would. Every Black leader in America knows where I've stood, and where I will stand when Black leaders are under attack. I asked Alton why I'm not good enough to be supported.

Alton responded by saying that he's defended me even when Rev hasn't, that he doesn't talk negatively about Fred, and that he never attacks me. I told him I needed more from him — that he needed to *defend* me. So then he said that it's not necessary to say everything, because the Black community would learn by what happens — for example, that Daniels couldn't get himself on the ballot in New York. Or that Daniels *talks* "Black, Black, Black" but then he showed up at the all-Black meeting at the Slave with a white man, which tipped the community off about how he was manipulating them with a Black nationalist politic when his campaign was really funded by white people.

I told Alton that I wasn't accusing him of anything, but that since he wouldn't speak out for me, I'd speak out for myself. I'm getting creamed, I told him, and many Black male leaders don't think it's necessary to stand up for me — despite the fact that some of them are the very same ones who say it's their job to defend Black womanhood. Alton said that he defends me in his own way and that I couldn't tell him when or how to do it.

I said, "Well, at least I know how to reach you. Since you won't answer my phone calls, I'll just get on the radio and talk about you!" He laughed. We have a friendly, principled relationship: there's no hostility between us, and we don't make false promises to one another.

6

MINISTER LOUIS FARRAKHAN: A MAN OF PRINCIPLE

He is a slender man, natty in his bow tie and gray suit, as clean-cut as a 1950s teen-ager at the high-school prom. But Louis Farrakhan is 50, a spellbinding orator whose incendiary brand of Black Muslim dogma, broadcast weekly from an ornate temple on Chicago's South Side, sounds like an echo from the days of Elijah Muhammad and Malcolm X — fiery stuff, replete with ominous prophecies of racial apocalypse and a black-supremacist millennium.

— NEWSWEEK, APRIL 23, 1984

Jesse Jackson disavowed June 28 anti-Semitic remarks made by Black Muslim leader Louis Farrakhan.

Farrakhan, in a radio speech June 24 from his Nation of Islam headquarters in Chicago, called Judaism a "gutter religion," the existence of Israel as a state "an outlaw act" and those who supported Israel, "criminals in the sight of almighty God."

Jackson, who was in the midst of a trip to Central America and Cuba, issued a statement from his headquarters in Washington saying he found such statements "reprehensible and morally indefensible."

"I disavow such comments and thoughts," Jackson said in the statement. "Minister Farrakhan hasn't participated in my cam-

paign in recent months because I discouraged his participation.
He isn't a part of our campaign."

— *FACTS ON FILE*, JUNE 29, 1984

I have the distinction of being one of the two Black leaders to have received the support of Louis Farrakhan in a run for national office. But unlike the other one, Jesse Jackson, I didn't turn around and kick the Minister in the teeth.

I've had dinner at the Palace, Minister Farrakhan's official residence in Chicago, several times. After a Nation of Islam public event he generally invites about 20 people to his house for dinner; it's an opportunity to spend intimate time with him. It's quite an honor. I get invited whenever I'm at an NOI gathering in Chicago.

The first time I heard Minister Farrakhan speak was more than 15 years before I actually met him. It was 1969, in Hempstead, Long Island, where I was a student at Hofstra University. He gave a talk on the relationship between Black men and women. It was very loving. He said Black women had to be protected. I was a budding feminist, so I felt conflicted. I was sort of intrigued by what he said, but I also felt very uncomfortable. I didn't want to be that kind of woman, dependent and under the care of a man. It was in complete opposition to what I thought a woman should be. I was fighting to make a different statement. I was constantly being told by Black men that I was too outspoken, too aggressive. I had opinions and positions. My reaction was that this was not for me.

I don't remember hearing the Minister speak again for many years. And I didn't hear much more about him or the Nation of Islam. I kept my distance: the NOI wasn't where I was — in graduate school, getting married, having my kids, living my life.

It's ironic that it was a Jew, Fred Newman, who reintroduced me to Minister Farrakhan. I had become more aware of the Minister again after the controversy surrounding his relationship to Jesse Jackson in 1984. Then, in 1985, when I was running for mayor of New York City on the New Alliance Party line, I had attracted the support of some local ministers of the Nation of Islam. That opened up contact between my campaign and the Muslim community, particularly Nation of Islam women. I was very moved by their support, and so it seemed only natural when Fred urged that I put out a very strong welcome to Minister Farrakhan, who was coming to New York to speak at Madison Square Garden. At the same time, local Black Democratic Party leaders — David Dinkins, who at the time was the Manhattan borough president (he became the mayor of New York City in 1990), and State Assemblyman Herman "Denny" Farrell — were obviously being told to repudiate him. Dinkins and Farrell held a press conference to announce that the Minister wasn't welcome in the city. Lorraine Stevens, who was then running for City Council president on the NAP ticket, and I did a press conference on the steps of City Hall with Jitu Weusi of the Black United Front and Father Lawrence Lucas, the radical priest who later became associated with the December 12th Coalition, to welcome Farrakhan. (The press conference was reported on in the newspapers, but Lorraine and I were cut out of the accompanying photographs.)

When Minister Farrakhan did come to New York, 20,000 people came out to see him. I was invited by the local ministers I knew to sit on the stage of the Garden during his address. Farrakhan personally greeted all of us when he came on stage, but he didn't know who I was. I sat on the stage for six hours. I had never been to one of the Nation's rallies before. It was an overwhelming — and intimidating — experience. I talked with Kwame Toure (formerly Stokely Carmichael, who later became the leader of the All-African People's Revolutionary Party), who was seated next to me. But mostly I was just trying to take it all in. When I'm intimidated I can become arrogant, which is what I did then — I kept my distance from the other Black leaders on the stage. Afterward Fred and I spoke about the need for me to participate in such situations as a grassroots leader — to take millions of people with me when I go as their representative. In those six hours I could have had 40 conversations.

Until then, my position toward Farrakhan had been shaped by our differences: I was an outspoken Black intellectual; I felt that the women in the NOI were oppressed, and I didn't want to support that. During that time Fred and I had many conversations about the need for me to conduct my relationship with Farrakhan on the basis of what was best for the Black community, not on who I thought was right and who was wrong. It was clear that in attacking Farrakhan, Dinkins and other Black Democrats (Mayor Tom Bradley of Los Angeles, for instance) were kowtowing to the white, often Jewish, voters or campaign bankrollers they relied on to keep them in office. My statement was unequivocal: I support the right of the Black community to choose its own leadership, even when there are strong differences between those leaders and me. I would speak out against attacks on Black leaders, and against any attempt to "repudiate" them.

Late in 1985, Michael Hardy and Bill Pleasant, two African American journalists and colleagues of mine, went to Chicago to conduct an extensive interview with the Minister for the

National Alliance newspaper, which was later reprinted as part of the book *Independent Black Leadership in America*. But I still had had no direct contact with Farrakhan.

Cuomo Demands Farrakhan Friend Join in TV Debate

— *NEW YORK POST*, OCTOBER 25, 1986

A number of NOI women worked on my campaign for mayor in 1985, but nothing much was said publicly about my relationship with Farrakhan's Nation of Islam until I ran for governor of New York in 1986. Then I was heavily attacked because of it. The opening shot was fired by the *New York Post* 10 days before the election, just after I had come back to New York City from being on a tour in Syracuse, New York. I was out on the street in Brooklyn campaigning when I got a message to call the office. All hell had broken loose when the *Post* published a piece about my connection to Farrakhan as a way to take a swipe at Governor Mario Cuomo, who two days earlier had called for my inclusion in a series of televised debates among the gubernatorial candidates. The New Alliance Party went from near invisibility (as far as the major media were concerned) to front-page headlines. It was great.

Cuomo had tried to use me in his re-election fight against his Republican challenger, Andrew O'Rourke, by insisting that I, the only African American and the only woman in the four-way race, be included in the debates. But the governor got a lot more than he bargained for. Overnight, the media white-out of my campaign came to an end; photographers and television crews were breaking down the doors to get pictures of the "anti-Semite" Cuomo had invited into the debates. The two right-wing candidates, O'Rourke and Right to Lifer Denis

Dillon, announced that they would not appear in a debate if I were present. Cuomo was now faced with the possibility of having to debate me one on one. Things got hotter still when the Jewish Defense League, a Zionist terrorist outfit, issued a series of death threats against me.

Then Cuomo sent me a hand-delivered letter. In it he asked me to "issue a clarification" of my relationship to Farrakhan — code words for, "If you want a career in the Democratic Party, sister, you'll repudiate Farrakhan." I don't know why, given my independent history, he thought I'd be interested in his offer. But then again, the New York Democratic Party was just getting to know me. And man, was I getting to know them!

I wrote back. In my letter I said that unlike all too many Black Democrats, I would not repudiate Minister Farrakhan because that would be the equivalent of repudiating my people — something I would *never, never do*. I urged the governor to stand up to the reactionaries in the race and participate in the debates. He didn't respond. That's the stand the liberals always take: ultimately, they won't go up against the right wing.

Meanwhile, I was thrown into the center of a media storm. The papers wrote endlessly about my intimate relationship with Louis Farrakhan — *to whom I had never actually spoken*. All I had done was to make a principled statement: the Black community has the right to choose its own leaders. That had made me, according to the *New York Post,* a "Farrakhan Friend." It also marked my coming of age as a political leader — not in a classroom but in the midst of major attacks by people who were both powerful and vicious. Those attacks were what taught me who Farrakhan was.

The death threats scared me. I had no idea if the JDL intended to kill me. Clearly, there were people who absolutely did not want me in the debates!

The death threats were so serious that I ended up having police escorts everywhere and stepping up my own security. I traveled like that for the last ten days of the campaign. It was nerve-wracking. I was always asking where my children, Amani and Ainka, were, given that this was going on. Amani, who was ten years old at the time, had heard about the controversy and the death threats on TV. I remember him asking me if somebody was going to murder me. I was upset, but I used the opportunity to teach him more about what I was doing, the importance of it, and the racists' response to it. "Black people get murdered just for walking down the street," I told him. "But that's not a reason not to fight."

Lenora Fulani, who led the radical New Alliance Party's effort to win ballot status by garnering 50,000 votes in the gubernatorial election fell far short of her goal. Party leaders said a week of free publicity courtesy of Gov. Mario Cuomo's request to include the controversial Fulani in a televised debate probably helped the party get slightly more than 25,000 votes, according to an unofficial tally. Four years ago, NAP's candidate for governor received about 5,200 votes.

— *GANNETT WESTCHESTER NEWS,* NOVEMBER 9, 1986

The Republicans and Democrats were trying to use Farrakhan's controversiality and (by association) mine to discourage support for independent politics. They didn't want to give me any credibility. They didn't want NAP to get ballot status. The attacks had an impact; they scared folks away from voting for me. We got 25,000 votes — half of what was needed for permanent ballot status — when we had been showing at 1% in the polls, which should have meant 50,000. So we were hurt. But we had established our unwillingness to compromise the Black community, which is at the heart of what NAP and I are all about.

The following year, as I began to travel around the country, I realized the impact all of this had had on the NOI membership. There aren't a lot of Black leaders willing to stand up and defend Farrakhan, to take the kind of heat and pay the kind of price that I had. In 1987 I flew to Buffalo for a college speaking engagement. When I got off the plane, the NOI minister was waiting for me. Brother Dennis Muhammad met me at the airport and provided security for me throughout the four days I was in the city. He and the other brothers from the NOI's security force, the Fruit of Islam, were conveying their appreciation for what I had done. That happened in other parts of the country as well. Over and over again I was told, "Minister Farrakhan told us to protect you."

As I was learning about the NOI, they were learning about me: a Black woman from New York who wouldn't back down. I was blown away by their response to me, a radical Black woman, a leader of a multi-racial organization who was outspokenly pro-gay and pro-Jewish. They were very respectful toward me — they had their positions and I had mine. Throughout 1987, if word got out that I was speaking in a city, NOI members would come out to hear me and publicly thank me for defending Farrakhan.

In March of 1988, Farrakhan and I appeared together at an event at the University of the District of Columbia which thousands of students attended. The event had originally been scheduled for February, Black History Month, but had been postponed in response to the commotion generated by people opposed to spending public funds on an event featuring Farrakhan, who was at that time being vilified in the press. But the Student Government Association and supportive members of the administration, including UDC president Rafael Cortada, prevailed, insisting on the right of academic freedom and the autonomy of their school.

I began to be invited to NOI events, which I attended whenever I could. (By that time my 1988 presidential campaign was underway.) Finally, at one event where the Minister himself was speaking, I went up to the dais and introduced myself to him. He was friendly and soft-spoken and said he'd seen me on TV and realized that I was a "humanist." I said that I wanted to speak to him about my presidential campaign, and he gave me his private telephone number. I called him and we met twice, once in Philadelphia and once in Baltimore. I soon got to know Farrakhan.

He was wonderful. I sort of fell in love with him. He was very decent, very smart, very open — a lovely human being. I was very honored to meet him. There's no way to meet this man and not love him. We definitely hit it off.

I was very anxious about representing NAP well in my meetings with him. I was eager for Farrakhan to understand why I was running for president as an independent. I wanted him to meet Fred. He asked me who Fred was in my life. I said that he was my political mentor, a dear friend, and very brilliant. Farrakhan agreed to meet Fred, but never has. We had a wonderful discussion about social therapy, the drug-free, radically humanistic clinical psychology that Fred began developing 20 years ago and that I practice. We talked about the therapy work I do in Harlem; I think he understood why social therapy — the work to create a new vision of who human beings are as individuals and as a species — is so important to our people.

It was in the course of those meetings with Minister Farrakhan that I realized I had to teach him, a religious leader,

about independent politics and its value to the Black community. That blew my mind. I wanted to convince him to come to
Atlanta, the site of the Democratic National Convention, where
I believed Black leaders needed to make a statement about the
party's rejection of Jesse Jackson and the need for African
Americans to go independent. At first he had not intended to be
there. I had told him that Jesse Jackson would be in Atlanta, trying to cut a deal with Michael Dukakis, and that if anyone could
unlock the minds of the African American community and open
up our people to the necessity of independent politics, he —
Farrakhan — could. I told him that our people needed him to
be in Atlanta. He really listened. He was very humble. Our discussions evolved into his decision to come to Atlanta, and became the basis of the electrifying talk he gave at his Black
Agenda conference at the Wheat Street Baptist Church.

After our meeting, he called me to say that he wanted to
have an event in Atlanta on the Black Agenda to which he
would invite all the presidential candidates and that he would
support whichever one of them supported the Black Agenda.
The day of the event — which was held on the Sunday afternoon before the Monday when the Democratic National
Convention opened — was one of the most moving experiences
of my life. Five thousand people were in the church that day.

The balcony was packed with reporters, Black and white.
The TV cameras were whirring. Some of the white reporters
had thrown a fit about having to be frisked by the Fruit of
Islam before being allowed to enter. But all the media wanted
to hear what Farrakhan was going to say. I spoke just before
Minister Farrakhan. Minister Akbar Muhammad, Farrakhan's
national representative, and Farrakhan were sitting right behind
me. The whole time that I was speaking Akbar was passing me
notes telling me to hurry up. Meanwhile, Farrakhan kept say-

ing, "Right on, Sister!" I told the crowd that Jesse Jackson, while a great leader, was now leading us to the wrong place, the Democratic Party. They all cheered.

Farrakhan's talk on the Black Agenda came directly out of our dialogues. It seemed to me that he understood clearly what was at stake. He made a very strong statement about me and what I was doing. I floated out of the church believing that Minister Farrakhan supported independent politics, that I'd have the support of the Nation of Islam, that the NOI would get the word out about my campaign throughout the country, and that I had sown the seeds of a relationship which would last a lifetime — a relationship that was very critical for Black people. Then I started to learn more about the Nation.

The next day I got a phone call on behalf of Brother Akbar and Brother Leonard Farrakhan Muhammad, Farrakhan's son-in-law. They wanted to meet with me. At the meeting they asked me if I really supported Minister Farrakhan. They quoted a statement of mine in which I said that anti-Jewish sentiment in the Black community ran high — for lawful reasons — and that while I didn't support it, I certainly understood it and understood that any seemingly anti-Jewish comments which Farrakhan might have made were simply a reflection of the attitudes of the larger Black community. They accused me of calling the Minister anti-Semitic. I felt like they were bullying me, and I became more and more upset. I asked them on whose behalf they had come. Had Minister Farrakhan sent them? They said no. At that point, I ended the meeting, telling them that if the Minister had anything to say to me, he would say it. Then I left. This meeting left me with the clear impression that everyone in a leadership position in the Nation didn't support me, or approve of the impact I was having on Minister Farrakhan.

Afterward I felt both intimidated and infuriated. I tried getting in touch with Farrakhan to talk it through. Someone conveyed to me that Farrakhan had designated Minister Abdul Alim Muhammad, the minister of the Washington, DC mosque, as his representative in our relationship. (Alim at that time was also the national spokesman for the NOI.) I had met Brother Alim at one of the meetings with Farrakhan and earned his respect. Throughout the '88 presidential campaign he was my channel to the Minister.

I reached Alim and I told him about the conversation with Leonard and Akbar. He said that some leaders of the Nation supported my relationship with Minister Farrakhan and others didn't. I felt as if some differences within the NOI that pre-dated my coming onto the scene were being exacerbated by my presence.

(Minister Alim and I have grown apart since my 1988 campaign. When he ran for Congress in 1990 he became involved with the neo-fascist Lyndon LaRouche, who was constantly looking for Black leaders through whom he could gain access to the Black community. The LaRouchites even organized in the Black community using Alim's name — he had openly praised LaRouche at a public event. Everywhere I went people were constantly asking me about it. I called Alim and asked him if he knew that LaRouche was a neo-fascist. "If you are going to work with white people," I told him, "these are not the ones." I called Farrakhan to tell him my concern about what this relationship with LaRouche projected about the Nation of Islam. Farrakhan said he hadn't known about it. Since this happened Alim and I haven't spoken.)

Meanwhile, I had spent most of June, the month before the 1988 Democratic convention, trying to reach Hosea Williams, an Atlanta city councilman and veteran civil rights activist; Gus Savage, then a congressman from Illinois; and Imamu Amiri

Baraka (the writer formerly known as LeRoi Jones), who were organizing one of the many protests that were taking place the week of the convention. I was going to Atlanta to protest the Democratic Party's treatment of Jesse Jackson and the Black community; I wanted to let Williams, Savage and Baraka know what I would be doing, but none of them would return my phone calls.

The march planned by Williams and Savage was scheduled for Monday, the first day of the convention. A rather large parking area, adjoining the convention center, had been designated as the official protest site. It was equipped with a stage and a sound system, and control of the stage was parceled out by the city in 45-minute blocks to any group that applied. There were many organizations participating in the Fulani protest, so by the time they completed filing for permits, it turned out that we controlled the stage and the demonstration area for the bulk of the four days. Alvaader Frazier, one of our attorneys, was in charge of the stage. For every slot we had, Alvaader would be on the site early, making sure that there would be no problems from the Democrats or the police or anyone else.

When I showed up on Monday afternoon for the march, which began at Dr. King's gravesite, Reverend Sharpton, Alton Maddox and the United African Movement were already there. So was the NOI. Williams and Savage were there, too. Things were confusing: at first there were two groups of marchers, going in different directions. I started marching with Sharpton and Maddox. Then one of Savage's aides invited me to join their contingent. I introduced myself to people in the crowd, and invited everyone to come back to the demonstration site after the march ended late that afternoon. We had the space reserved at the end of the day and I wanted all of the leaders to end up on the stage together so we could have a major rally.

Eventually the two groups began going in the same direction; at different times I marched at the head of both.

Two thousand people came back to the demonstration site for a rally. The leaders went up on the stage: Hosea Williams; the Reverend Charles Koen of Cairo, Illinois; Minister Alim and other representatives of the NOI; Reverend Sharpton; Tawana Brawley, the young woman who had been raped by a gang of whites in upstate New York; Alton Maddox; Amiri Baraka; Gus Savage; and the Reverend Ben Chavis, formerly of the Wilmington 10 and later a member of the United Church of Christ's Commission on Racial Justice. The site was packed. Alvaader Frazier, who was on the job onstage, handed me the mike and I began to welcome people.

Suddenly, Hosea was whispering to me, "Give me the mike!"

At first I thought he was joking and I kept talking. When I realized he wasn't, I said into the mike, "Wait a minute." He tried to grab it from me. I told him to stop. We ended up wrestling for it — a match that was broadcast on coast-to-coast television! The crowd was yelling at him to leave the mike alone. The people standing closest to the stage asked me if I needed help and started chanting my name. I wouldn't let the mike go. Hosea was furious. Everybody else on the stage was just standing there, dumbstruck.

In the end, I won the wrestling match. Holding on to the microphone, I told the crowd that the Democrats had sabotaged Jesse's campaign. He wasn't going to get the nomination; it was time to take the second, independent road. The crowd clapped. Then Hosea took the mike, while whispering to me that I had stolen his march.

Hosea and the Black Democrats didn't like what I had to say. His statement — which was echoed by Savage and Baraka — was that the Democratic Party was not being fair to the Black community. They said the DP was not supporting the Black Agenda, that Jesse should be the vice presidential nominee — but that ultimately Black people should vote for Dukakis anyway. In other words, they were putting out a lot of rhetoric but they had no balls. It was a sham. They weren't putting out any ultimatum to the Democratic Party. It wasn't a serious statement.

After the crowd saw that the men had attempted to manhandle me, each time a speaker took the mike the people checked to see if it was okay with me. At one point the crowd booed Ben Chavis. He threw down the mike and walked off the stage.

Hosea was furious that I had come to his march and "grabbed" the people. When he got the mike, he kept saying, "Don't worry. I'm going to give the mike to Dr. Fulani but I'm leaving." He obviously expected the crowd to leave with him, but only a handful of people did. I believe they stayed because the political statement I was making made the most sense.

Meanwhile, Baraka had gotten hold of a second mike and was yelling at the crowd. I wasn't going to allow him to abuse the marchers, so I gave instructions to shut that mike off. At some point in the middle of all this, Reverend Sharpton had walked off the stage, taking Tawana Brawley with him. I sent for Rev to come back because I thought it was important for him to speak. I also wanted Minister Alim to address the crowd. In that disciplined and dignified way that Muslims carry themselves, the minister told me it wasn't "necessary." I said, "Yes, it is." Alim put out the same pro-independent statement that Minister Farrakhan had made the day before at Wheat Street. He obviously didn't share the position taken by Akbar and Leonard.

At the end, Reverend Koen (who would later go to jail on trumped-up charges that he had burned down his own headquarters in order to embezzle the insurance money) asked me if he could give the closing prayer. I said yes. At the close of this fracas, everybody held hands while he prayed for unity.

Of course, word of all this got out on the floor of the Democratic convention in a matter of minutes. One story going around was that I had thrown ketchup on Ben Chavis! Everyone heard that Hosea and I had had a fight and that I'd won.

I *had* won: Hosea Williams and Co. found out that I wasn't going anywhere. The pro-Democratic Party Black leadership couldn't shut us up. I would be there and I would represent the independent position in the Black community. It wasn't a petty fight. I've been trying to get these brothers to have this debate for a very long time — *not* having the debate protects the Democratic Party.

That same day, Fred Newman was approached by Walid Muhammad, the editor of the *Final Call* and some other NOI leaders, who said they didn't like how the Black Agenda event at the Wheat Street Baptist Church had been covered in the *National Alliance* newspaper (Fred's one of the editors). The headline to which they objected was: "Farrakhan, Fulani Present Black Agenda — Where's Jesse?" which they said falsely portrayed Farrakhan and me as close allies. Fred responded that all of the presidential candidates had been invited and I was the only one who came. The coverage, he said, was accurate. (Walid, who has since died, was rather traditional. Once, in an interview, he asked me when I was going to get married and start baking bean pies.)

Mid-1960s Bureau documents lay heavy stress on the "violently antiwhite" character of the NOI, and both the organization and Elijah Muhammad were targeted for special attention when the Bureau established a "Black Nationalist Hate

Group" COINTEL [counter-intelligence — LBF] program in
1967 and 1968. The Bureau also had a strong interest in other
Muslim leaders, such as Malcolm X, and played assorted
COINTEL tricks on the organization as early as the late 1950s.

— THE FBI AND MARTIN LUTHER KING, JR.,
BY DAVID GARROW, 1981

Many people in the NOI believe it should be a religious organization, period. My own opinion is that religious organizations
are extremely political. Others in the NOI who are uncomfortable with me argue that Jesse Jackson spat in the face of
Farrakhan and the Muslim community after the Minister
reached out to Jesse in 1984 and publicly supported his first
presidential campaign; they don't want the Minister to support
another political leader and take that risk again. That sentiment
fuels the arguments of people who never wanted the NOI to be
involved in politics in the first place. Then there are people inside the NOI who support the Democratic Party, and who
don't like me because they see me as a threat to the Democratic
Party's relationship to the Black community.

There is also a lot of support within the Nation for me;
many people were thrilled that the Minister had embraced me.

I didn't see Minister Farrakhan or speak to him again until
mid-August, when we were — by coincidence — both in St.
Louis at the same time; the NOI was hosting a talk there by the
Minister and I was in town as part of a 30-city tour to take out
the Black Agenda.

I decided to stop by to hear the Minister after I came back
from my own speaking engagement. I walked into the reception hosted in his honor and I got on the receiving line so that
I could say hello to him. Brother Akbar came over and said he
wanted to speak to me; I went to a table with him and we sat

down. He told me that the Minister didn't want to speak with me and that I should not approach him. I didn't believe him, and said so. He threatened to call out the Fruit of Islam guards who were present in the room. I looked him straight in the eye. "I'm going to speak to Minister Farrakhan tonight, Brother — that's what I have to do," I said. "And you should do whatever you have to do." Then I got back on the reception line.

When I reached him, the Minister must have seen how upset I was. He hugged me, then took me over to a table. I told him what Akbar had done, and that I had been trying unsuccessfully for months to reach him. I asked him what was going on. "If you don't want to speak with me, tell me and tell me why," I said. He conveyed to me that there were things he needed to work out, but that if I ever needed to speak with him I should do so.

I sat in the audience to hear his address. Although he didn't mention my name, and didn't refer explicitly to what had just happened, he made it the subject of his talk. He spoke about the difficulties that Black organizations have in working together, about divisiveness, about the need to move beyond that, and about the role that he could play in bringing about unity. It was very moving.

But rumors about my posture toward him continued to fly. It was being said that I had called the Minister anti-Semitic. The rumor mongers were citing my statement from my 1986 gubernatorial campaign in which I laid out the differences I had with Minister Farrakhan on a number of issues, insisting on my right to disagree with an African American leader without having to — and in fact refusing to — repudiate him. I became worried about becoming the lightning rod for the tensions within the NOI. I didn't want to be in this position in what I felt was a dangerous situation. I knew that

Malcolm X was killed because the opportunistic enemies of Black people had capitalized on the fights taking place within the NOI in his day. In 1988 I was concerned about the powers-that-be thinking that there were serious differences within the Nation from which they could derive an advantage. I felt concerned about being used to create problems for Minister Farrakhan. This is a dangerous business; I did not want anything to happen to him!

I felt that the rumors were dangerous for both of us. In the next few weeks, I shared my concerns with Minister Alim. I wanted to put out a statement to the press to dispel the rumors, to make clear where I was coming from, and to short circuit the current of disruption that was flowing inside the NOI. In September of 1988 Alim came to New York and we did a press conference together on the steps of City Hall. Minister Alim made an eloquent statement of support for my campaign, and I once again reaffirmed my support for Minister Farrakhan while also strongly insisting that Black leaders — like white leaders — have the right to have differences without having to repudiate each other.

I was traveling around the country a lot that year; I went to hear Farrakhan speak whenever we were in the same city. For the most part he was cordial — but although Alim continued to work with me, the Minister kept his distance from my presidential campaign.

Reverend Sharpton, Alton Maddox and I met with Farrakhan several times in 1989 and 1990. During one of those meetings — both Rev and Alton were there — Farrakhan spoke of his great love and respect for me and encouraged me to continue the work that I was doing because it was important for our people. He wanted me to know that he was there for me.

On another occasion, in 1990, the Minister said that he had

been "negligent" in his relationship to me and wanted to do something about it. I invited him to come to New York to endorse my gubernatorial campaign that year, which he did. Reverend Sharpton played a crucial role in making that happen. My perspective was that Minister Farrakhan, Reverend Sharpton and I were the three most independent Black leaders in America, and that it was critical to engage in a collective effort on behalf of the Black community.

The press conference at which Farrakhan formally endorsed me for governor was held at the Grand Hyatt Hotel in Manhattan on October 17, 1990. Although many reporters were there, including all of the Black press, it got relatively little coverage. After the press conference, Rev and the Minister and I spent some time talking in his hotel suite. It was very cordial. But it turned out to be the last time I would see or speak to Farrakhan for the duration of my gubernatorial run.

It seemed to me that each time Farrakhan took two steps forward, he took three steps back; he would come out very powerfully, then retreat. It was as if he were apologizing for his closeness to me. I believe the Minister meant everything he said to me, but he runs an organization which includes among its leadership people who are vehemently opposed to the NOI and NAP coming closer.

Farrakhan knew that I was running for president again in 1992. People used to call in to radio talk shows all the time when I was on the air during that year to ask me where he stood on my independent presidential campaign. I told them to ask him. I've taken a lot of heat for defending controversial Black leaders. In 1992 the question was: were these brothers ready to take some heat for supporting me?

I ran into Minister Farrakhan at a party given by the Libyan mission to the UN in September, just five weeks or so before election day. He asked me to call him at home in Chicago, which I did. In that call I told him about the attacks coming down on me. I said I expected other Black leaders to come out and defend me. He promised to do what he could.

There have been times when I've been disappointed that Farrakhan wouldn't take a public stand on what he's said to me in private. But I believe he's limited in what he can do in terms of giving support to independent politics. I feel sad about that — because he's a brilliant spokesperson for the plight of Black people. He has something to give, and it needs to be given, among other places, in the political arena. I think he knows that — but for many complex reasons he can't do it. I understand.

There are a lot of things that keep Minister Farrakhan and me apart, although on the occasions when we find ourselves together it's as if we talked every day. With all of our differences, I love him very dearly.

7

PRO-GAY
365 DAYS A YEAR

I am your sexual preference!

— MY SLOGAN AT THE
1992 GAY PRIDE MARCH IN NEW YORK CITY

NAP has marched in the Gay Pride parade in New York City for years. We used to appear in matching T-shirts, marching in step. We were making a point about working-class (and gay) militancy. But I had always wanted to go to the Gay Pride parade dressed up.

For 1992 we had a beautiful float which carried me (wearing the sexiest dress I've ever worn), rapper M.C. Browneyes from the All Stars Talent Show Network, Fred Newman, men in drag, women in drag. Our slogan was "Fulani for Prez: She's a sexual preference." Once we hit the Village, the crowds lining the streets cheered. They were yelling, "Go ahead, girl!" They loved it.

The New Alliance Party was pro-gay from *before* it was founded. But that's not the initial reason I started working with NAP.

I was attracted to the New Alliance Party because it was in the Black community and because it had a serious relationship with the Black poor. Not only were Black people active leaders of NAP, so were gay people. Gay people came with the turf, and as I grew politically I learned (among other things) about the gay issue. I learned a lot by virtue of going with what NAP was.

I came out of the nationalist movement, which was homo-phobic as hell. The people in the movement who were thought to be gay were allowed to be there — but they had to stay in the closet. It was a very macho environment, and no one — in-cluding me — ever challenged the homophobia openly. But once I began working with NAP, I learned quickly.

NAP events were always multi-racial and multi-sexual. I was mostly used to all-Black crowds, at least in terms of partying and hanging out. At first I was uncomfortable with everything. I had conflicts about everything. I mostly identified my con-flicts with moving into a multi-racial milieu. It took two and a half years for me to commit myself to NAP. I'm sure that along with my resistance to multi-racialism my conflicts about work-ing with gay people made it take me so long.

I came to Hofstra University as a freshman in 1968. On campus the Black men were being "real men," and the word was that Black women had to step back in order to "support their men." We were told that if we were too outspoken, if we provided too much leadership, it would hold back the men. We were asked — commanded, really — to stifle our development so the men could develop. We were supposed to help make up for the 400 years that Black men had been oppressed. The movement was organized on the premise that the brothers had to lead it. This premise was plainly anti-woman — but that wasn't at all clear to me at first.

As a freshman I was conflicted about it. I've always been outspoken. I had been very active in my church. I was an officer in my high school. I was a young leader.

So I had a hard time putting a lid on, or playing second fiddle. Looking back, I guess I thought the "request" was temporary — so I figured I would do it for a year or so. I also began dating the guy who was elected the head of the Black student organization, so I was somewhat elevated in my oppression.

When I was there the gay people on Hofstra's campus — Black and white — were invisible. That's a measure of the degree of homophobia that existed. They were invisible to me, too. What I reacted to most in the nationalist movement was the sexism (which, of course, is very related to homophobia).

The nationalist line is that there are no homosexuals in Africa, that homosexuality is a "white man's disease" and that, to the extent that there are Black homosexuals here, it's a result of their being tainted by European culture. The nationalist movement uses the word "faggot" with the same frequency and casualness that the Klan uses the word "nigger." It's used so much that most of the time it's not even uttered from a fighting stance. That word was all over the movement and got used to put down both gay people and women. In the minds of the men "faggot" meant a man who acts like women. But I was only dimly aware of all that then.

When I came around NAP, there was, of course, a very different attitude — NAP was *pro-gay* and actively fighting homophobia. There were white people, Jews, lesbians and gay men working at every level of leadership in the party.

I remember working the most, at first, on my anti-Semitism. I came to realize that a lot of the common, everyday, familiar stuff that I had learned about Jews was deeply anti-Semitic. I had to deal with the contradiction of feeling very close politically and personally to Fred and other Jewish organizers and recognizing that what I had learned about them was a pile of bull and very hurtful. I worked aggressively to do something about that.

I think I had more of a handle on my homophobia — I understood it more and was more sensitive around it than around anti-Semitism. When you're conscious of something you can deal better with it — you don't act out on it. I'm not sure why I was sensitive about homophobia. It probably had to do with the connection between sexism and homophobia and also because of some experiences in my early life.

One of my cousins was a gay man. He committed suicide when he was 24. At the hospital they said he had taken an overdose, but he was driven to it by the homophobic way my family related to him.

They didn't take him seriously. I don't remember what they said; I remember the posture, the attitude toward him. They had this notion that there was something wrong with him. He faced a lot of ridicule.

I was eight years old when my cousin's mother went out one day to get some cold cuts for my uncle's lunch and never came back. When they found her a few days later, it turned out that white men had raped and probably beaten her and then tied her to railroad tracks; the train killed her. No one was ever punished for the murder.

After that my uncle became an alcoholic and a recluse. A year after my aunt was killed, my mother and father and my grandmother and grandfather bought a house together and my uncle lived with us for a while. He was my favorite uncle. I loved him dearly and we had a strong relationship. He raised his kids the best he could, but his whole family was destroyed by tragedy. His two boys were left alone in the house a lot. There was constant craziness.

When my cousin died, no one seemed to mourn, no one grieved. I can't even remember if I went to his funeral. As a kid I felt so pained by that, even though I didn't know what "that" was. It stayed with me. It was one of those things that happen which shape you emotionally. When I got older I realized that he had been gay.

Another homophobic incident which had a big impact on me when I was young had to do with the man who directed our church choir. (I played the piano at my church from the time I was 12 until I was 18.) Everybody sort of knew he was gay, but nobody said anything about it until they decided to replace him so that they could do something else with his salary line. They used his homosexuality as an excuse to get rid of him. I was 15 or 16 and I was enraged by that. I went to bat for him, fighting for him to remain the choir director.

I went to a prayer meeting and confronted my minister about the situation. He wasn't talking about it; he was covering up what was going on. I was really furious. Other young people followed my lead and rallied to the choir director's side, but he lost his job anyway. My mother's response was, "Why can't you go to prayer meetings and pray like everyone else?"

I think that these things sensitized me. But that's not to say that I was never homophobic or that I was outspoken about gay rights before I met NAP. I wasn't.

NAP's position on gayness goes beyond the usual liberal/left attitude that "what you do in the privacy of your own bedroom is your business." NAP says that gayness is a radical political choice (although not necessarily a conscious choice on the part of the individual), a positive rebellion against oppressive and abusive sex roles.

We believe that homosexuality is neither biologically determined, nor is it a free (personal) choice. Being gay includes the organization of sexual desires and needs as well as fighting for certain political rights, but it can't be reduced to any of these things in themselves. Separating the personal and the political is

the rule in our society, particularly when it comes to understanding things that are emotional (and considered internal)
and things that are social (and considered external). Gayness is
neither personal nor political; rather, we constantly have to explore the *relationship* between how we express our emotionality
and sexuality and what's happening in the rest of the world, because our sexuality is determined by that relationship — it
doesn't operate independently, as a thing in itself.

Our society, as it is currently organized, is sexually, socially
and politically repressive. The attempt to break out of this repression by living one's life as a gay man or woman is not
"evil," as the far right preaches. Nor is it genetically determined, as more and more of the gay establishment is insisting.
And it isn't crazy, as the psychologists have long maintained. It
is a positive, socially progressive way of life and part of the *natural* process of human social development — and therefore
profoundly human.

Yet gay people are increasingly attacked as unnatural and
anti-human. The anti-gay resolutions that were on the ballot in
Oregon and Colorado in 1992 are just the tip of the iceberg.
Gays are blamed — along with Blacks, Latinos, Jews, women,
poor people and the other "minorities" which make up the majority of the world — for the decadence and decay of late 20th
century capitalism. The right — which has seized control of the
Republican Party — has built a mass movement to give legiti-
macy to a social climate in which the quarantine or outright
elimination of homosexuals is being openly demanded.

In NAP's critique of the traditional left (and traditional nationalism, for that matter) we have raised over and over again
their unwillingness to deal seriously with the question of human
development — with sexuality, with morality, with questions
like "What is a man?" "What is a woman?" The left has con-

fined itself to the traditional, and very narrow, concerns of "politics" and "economics." But if you're serious about a new humanistic movement — a new America, a new world — then you have to deal with questions of human development, including the development of morality. You can't leave these things to be taken over by the right because their morality is anti-human and anti-developmental.

Understanding that has allowed NAP to take a more radical stance relative to gay rights than the traditional left does. The left's position is to "tolerate" different people, at best to stand up for the "right" of people to be "different." As a result, the left is into *tokenism* as much as (if not more than) any other institution in this country.

NAP's position is not one of "tolerance" — it's one of radical restructuring, including the restructuring of what it means to be a human being.

Just as our positions and perspective on who the African American people are grew out of extensive organizing in the Black community, NAP's positions and perspective on who gay people are comes out of extensive organizing in the gay community. In the context of organizing in these communities we've had a lot of fights with both Black nationalists and gay separatists, fights which informed and shaped our understanding of these communities and their role in the historic struggle to transform the world.

When NAP started it went directly into the poor Black community and into the gay community. It didn't join existing Black and gay organizations which were controlled by the Democratic Party or which mediated the relationship between the community and the Democratic Party. That we located ourselves in those oppressed communities decisively shaped NAP's character; it determined who was to be included and who was to lead.

Many Black and Latino gays and lesbians from the South Bronx got involved in NAP's very first campaign — when State Senator Joseph Galiber ran for Bronx borough president in 1979. (He came in first in the predominantly Black and Puerto Rican South Bronx and second overall.)

It was the first time that most of these sisters and brothers had ever been involved in politics. Vera Hill, who was one of my first and dearest friends in NAP, and who has taught me so much about our history, is one of NAP's lesbian leaders who emerged during the Galiber campaign.

The Lesbian and Gay Task Force of NAP and the New York City Union of Lesbians and Gay Men grew out of the Galiber campaign. The first thing the Task Force did after it was formed was to organize a contingent to take part in the first National March on Washington for Lesbian and Gay Rights. They distributed a position paper, "Now is the Time to Go Independent" and gathered signatures on a petition calling for the formation of an independent union of lesbians and gay men which would represent them in making demands on decision-making bodies, businesses and elected officials in the gay community. The response was overwhelming.

The New York City Union of Lesbians and Gay Men was founded by these organizers in the months after they got back from Washington. It became a political voice for Black, Latino and working-class gays and lesbians who had never been wanted by the middle class-dominated gay rights movement, challenging its Democratic Party-controlled leadership at every turn. The official gay leaders have hated NAP ever since.

The Union was the first lesbian and gay organization to come out against former Mayor Ed Koch, a "neo-liberal" racist; it was the only gay organization in the Coalition to Defeat Koch, a coalition led by the Black United Front, the

Metropolitan Council on Housing and the New Alliance Party. In 1981 the Union worked hard on the independent mayoral campaign of Brooklyn Assemblyman Frank Barbaro — who ran against Koch in the Democratic primary and then (reluctantly) as an independent on the Unity Party line. (Other gay organizations supported Koch after it became apparent that he would win.) The Union also took the fight to pass a Gay Rights Bill in New York City into the streets, launching a petitioning drive to mobilize support for it in September 1980. (The bill wasn't passed until 1985.)

By working closely with the African American and Puerto Rican communities, the Union was challenging the phony separatism of the gay movement. I say phony because most of the leadership of the gay movement, while it may have talked a militant separatist line, was more than willing to work with the straight-dominated and thoroughly homophobic Democratic Party. At the same time, the Union played an important role in keeping the fight against homophobia in the forefront of NAP's concerns.

We needed to find out who in the middle-class gay community was willing to follow the leadership of poor gays, of Black and Latino gays, of transvestites and transsexuals. The gay community has its own hierarchy: according to middle-class white gay men, poor people, people of color, and transvestites don't do gayness "right." The development of Vera Hill and her sisters and brothers from the working-class gay community as leaders of the New Alliance Party directly challenged all that nonsense.

Eventually the existence of a separate gay organization within NAP began to undermine both our ability to integrate gay people into the New Alliance Party *and* our ability to organize in the gay community. The Union — by enclosing gay supporters of independent politics off into a separate organization — had erected a wall between our gay and straight members and was actually preventing our gay activists from providing leadership to all the party's activities. Breaking down the wall allowed us to advance both our positions on gayness and our relationship to the gay community.

We put the demand on our gay members to provide leadership to *all* our work and to *all* people. That raised serious issues for some gay organizers because they — like all oppressed people in our society — were so used to being related to as tokens. Some of them left NAP, but the end of the Union ushered in a period of growth for us in the gay community.

Another organization which played an important role in the evolution of NAP's relationship to the gay community and in the relationship between the gay community and poor communities of color was the Coalition of Grassroots Women. The Coalition was launched in the late '70s by a group of Black, Latina and Asian women who had been iced out of the middle-class women's movement. The founders were all significant working-class leaders, including Geraldine Miller of Bronx Household Technicians, Margaret Prescott Roberts of Black Women for Wages for Housework, Beulah Saunders of the National Welfare Rights Organization, Marissa de los Andes of Mujeres Internacionales por la Liberación Americana, and Kuzu Iyiama of the Organization of Asian Women.

In 1977, the path of the CGRW crossed that of *Don't Mourn, Organize!*, a communications bulletin of grassroots organizations which was edited by Freda Rosen — a longtime lesbian activist who would go on to become a leader of the New Alliance Party. Recognizing Freda's skills as a mass organizer, Marissa de los Andes appealed to *Don't Mourn, Organize!* for help in building a base in working-class communities.

As the Coalition began to organize poor women, radical

lesbians (many of them from working-class backgrounds) who had been purged from the official women's movement became attracted to its work. In 1979 two leaders of the Feminist Women's Health Center of Tallahassee, Linda Curtis and Kit Davis, who had heard of Freda through the *Don't Mourn, Organize!* network, came to New York City to work with the Coalition and stayed on to become founders of NAP. (In 1992 Curtis managed my campaign in Virginia and Texas and later became the chief organizer of the New Alliance Party in Texas.)

A number of lesbian activists from around the country soon followed in their footsteps. Many of them would go on to become leaders of the political tendency that gave birth to NAP. From Oregon came Nomi Azulay, who in 1982 became NAP's first openly gay candidate (she ran for City Council in District 3 in the Greenwich Village area), and the first openly gay person to run for public office in New York City.

Dr. Susan Massad, then the director of the Outpatient Clinic at Jacobi Hospital in the Bronx, succeeded Freda Rosen as the coordinator of the CGRW. In the mid-'80s she went on to establish health clinics for the New York Institute for Social Therapy in Harlem and the Bronx. In 1989, when Adam Abdul-Hakeem (formerly known as Larry Davis) was being beaten and terrorized by prison guards (in retaliation for his having publicly accused corrupt police officers of recruiting young Black and Puerto Rican men to run drugs for them), Dr. Massad served as his personal physician and helped to save his life.

Kate Gardner from Washington state pioneered NAP's public relations operation. She later became the director of the Rainbow Lobby in Massachusetts during the period when it helped to spearhead the passage of Question #4, a major ballot-access reform referendum which reduced the number of signatures required of independent candidates by 75%, gave voters the right to register in parties other than the Democratic and Republican parties and allowed an organization to become a ballot-status party by registering 1% of the voters or by gaining 3% of the vote for any statewide office.

Mary Fridley had been producing women's music concerts in the Midwest before she came to New York to work with the Coalition of Grassroots Women; she went on to become one of the independent movement's top fundraisers as well as a talented social therapist.

Some of the Coalition's founders, who had themselves come under attack from the middle-class women's movement, weren't happy with the growing numbers of white lesbians who were becoming involved in the CGRW; they were afraid that the organization was being "taken over" by leftists and lesbians. At a conference in Oberlin, Ohio, Wilmet Brown called Rosen a "leftist man in drag." But Freda and the others from *Don't Mourn, Organize!* didn't back down an inch in defending the right of lesbian women to participate in and lead the organization. While some of its founders deserted the Coalition, most of the rank-and-file members supported the lesbians and CGRW's thrust toward grassroots organizing.

The Coalition went on to rebuild the Bronx Coalition Against Sterilization Abuse, and to organize the Clinton Union of Community Women and the Working Women's Sisterhood. It also became — along with the Labor Community Alliance for Change, the New York City Unemployed and Welfare Council, the National Federation of Independent Unions and other groups — a founding organizational member of the New Alliance Party.

That historic clash between radical white lesbians and poor women of color — and the unique and very powerful unity which emerged from it — was an important moment in the development of what was to become the New Alliance Party political tendency. It set a precedent which helped shape what NAP would be.

NAP challenges backward and reactionary politics no matter who's articulating them. We've never gone into the poor community and said, "Whatever your positions are, that's what we'll support." Our job is to provide leadership. The New Alliance Party puts out what we think is in the interests of poor and working people *as a whole* and people have to decide what they want to do with that.

We're not liberals. That confuses many people because the only progressives they've ever known — even the ones who called themselves communists — were liberals. That's why a lot of folks tend to conflate principledness with liberalism. We're principled, but we're not liberal. We never cater to backwardness and never back down in the face of racism, homophobia, sexism and anti-Semitism — no matter where the attacks are coming from.

I support Jim Mangia because he represents the true alliance, an alliance based on self interest but not greed, on self advancement but not power-mongering.

— REVEREND AL SHARPTON,
NATIONAL ALLIANCE, SEPTEMBER 27, 1990

I'm probably the only straight Black leader in the country who gets gay-baited. I had some intense fights in the Black community about NAP's pro-gay commitment.

A few years ago we did a series of conferences on "Blacks and Gays" in Harlem. I remember going on a radio show with a local Black minister. In the middle of the show he realized I was putting out a pro-gay position. He began talking about

Sodom and Gomorrah, so I took him on. We had a major fight on the air; it was wonderful.

A lot of Black men walk up to me on the street in Harlem to tell me that if I gave up my pro-gay stance they'd join NAP. When I walk past the Black Hebrews, a right-wing religious nationalist group which holds street corner rallies, they start screaming, "Here comes Fulani, the Black lesbian bitch."

The December 12th Coalition — a group of self-proclaimed revolutionary Black nationalists — are also vicious gay-baiters. When eight of their leaders were arrested in a Gestapo-style raid back in 1984 (at the time they called themselves the New York 8+), the New Alliance Party and I gave them substantial political and material support. By their own account, we were one of the few organizations that did. However, they broke with us after we criticized Father Lawrence Lucas, an ally of theirs, for saying during a press conference that there was "no one to vote for" in the 1985 mayoral election. (I was an independent candidate for mayor and happened to be standing next to him on the steps of City Hall at the time!)

The New York 8+ quickly grew nasty. I remember one incident in particular — it was a citywide rally against Koch outside his Greenwich Village townhouse. As the NAP contingent unfurled its "Boycott the Democratic Party" banner, the December 12th "security squad" under orders from Coltrane Chimurenga tried (unsuccessfully, thanks to support from many of the demonstrators) to get us to put the banner down. Later, when the leadership of the rally refused to allow me on stage, people in the crowd began chanting, "Let Fulani speak!" Chimurenga again sicked his goon squad on me, on Pam Lewis, a Black lesbian who at that time was the New York state coordinator of NAP, and on other NAP organizers in an attempt to throw us out — an attempt that failed after much pushing and shoving as others from the crowd surged forward to defend us.

After the unsuccessful attempt to eject me and the New Alliance Party from the rally, Lisa Williamson — who would become better known as Sister Souljah — began to attack me verbally from the stage. She accused me of being controlled by Zionists — a strange charge since it was right-wing Zionists who had threatened my life during my gubernatorial race the year before. What she really meant, of course, was Jews. Then she went off on the "faggots" in the New Alliance Party. Included in her diatribe was the following statement: "We have to get definition and then we get unified and we march ahead. We love each other, man for woman, woman for man, to bring forth children, to bring forth soldiers, in a war that's being waged against us."

Sister Souljah and Chimurenga and the Black Hebrews and the other gay-baiters who "accuse" me of being a "gay lover" (I am proud to plead guilty!) are actually paying me and NAP an extraordinary compliment. What they can't believe is that anyone who's not gay could be pro-gay when being gay carries such a stigma in our society. They can't believe that anyone who is oppressed would defend another oppressed group. But that's exactly what NAP is about — the despised and the left-out working together. What we're building is an organization of the excluded — and you can't be more excluded than a gay person of color.

Over the last few months our coalition partners in the independent political movement have warned me, "You have to be careful that you don't get identified as fringe."

But the reality is that you *must* be identified as fringe if you're going out to organize poor people of color and lesbians and gays. In our society they're illegitimate. If they make up the bulk of your membership and leadership, as they do in NAP, then people will relate to you as fringe. And that's what we have to challenge. We don't want to be more legitimate on the terms of this oppressive society. There's nothing I can do about NAP being fringe in this way because that's what we *want* it to be. We knew from the beginning that if you want to build a truly independent movement in this country there are particular communities you're going to have to organize. That's what we mean when we say we are Black-led, multiracial and pro-gay.

That raises particular issues for Black men, especially if they're out to make it. They feel that they have enough strikes against them; it would be self-defeating to be identified with other oppressed groups.

Reverend Sharpton is one African American male leader who has been open enough to learn about homophobia from me. I think it's because his commitment to liberating the oppressed is stronger than the attitudes and prejudices he learned from the nationalist movement.

One way that I've had an impact on Rev is that when I go into nationalist meetings — such as when I used to speak to the United African Movement at the Slave or at his more recent meetings of the National Action Network in Harlem, or wherever — I speak of *all* the constituencies which make up the New Alliance Party and I don't leave out the gay community. When people get finished cringing I think they hear that I stand for something, that I'm building something with gay people. That doesn't mean they like it or agree with it, but I think they respect it. It's clear that I'm making a particular statement about the importance of the gay community.

It's not, for example, that I'm trying to organize the Nation of Islam to become a gay organization; what I'm saying to them is that this is the humane position. This is the progressive position. And this is NAP's position. This is who we are. If you want me here, this is who I come as.

Organizing gay people to march with us for racial justice as we did in Bensonhurst, in Teaneck, in Los Angeles and lots of other places had an impact. We had our fights in those marches; we said, "You don't have to walk next to this person, you don't have to like this person, but you can't mess with them, either."

Black people, including nationalists, are attracted to NAP's work and at some point they have to come to terms with who's doing the work that's so powerful — and it's all of us, including our gay and lesbian members and leaders.

Rev has often come to NAP meetings. He is quite familiar with our openly pro-gay politics. By the time I invited him to come with me to the Castro in San Francisco and support the campaign of Jim Mangia, a leader of the California Peace and Freedom Party and of NAP who was running as an openly gay candidate for the San Francisco Board of Supervisors in 1990, we had been through an extended political process together. Rev was developing as a more broad-based political leader and he recognized that you can't do that if you make statements in opposition to other groups of people.

It was very moving to take Rev to the Castro. The gay Democrats were on hand to heckle when he and I campaigned for Jim there. I told them they couldn't, because it was homophobic. "I don't care if you're the gayest person in the world," I said. "Not embracing a Black civil rights leader, not coming closer to him, is anti-gay." The gay community needs to open up the struggle to everybody if it wants to win — and it needs especially to embrace a leader such as Reverend Sharpton, who acknowledged that in concentrating on the struggle against racism he has not done all he could do in the arena of gay rights and was there to change that.

Rev talked that day in the Castro about the failure of Black leadership to address the AIDS epidemic because they considered it a "gay disease," and the importance of turning that around. He also talked about what he had learned from me and our political movement about doing something different as a Black leader.

In the course of working with us Rev has met many lesbian and gay leaders of NAP in addition to Jim and gotten to know them as real people and as committed revolutionaries.

I've learned from our movement how to be very upfront about who we are — you just put it out and people have to deal with their reactions to it. That's why the gay community respects me; in situations where it would be easier to say nothing, I include them.

Recently the gay-baiting has let up a bit. People don't take me on about it much anymore. I think it's become clear that I won't back down, and that they can't use it to ridicule me or anything that I do. I've used the fights to bring the issue of homophobia out to the Black community, to challenge people's assumptions and prejudices. I talk about my support of gay people on Black radio stations like WLIB and WWRL all the time. I just do it. They've gotten vicious phone calls, but the cowards usually call in after I leave the studio.

One of the first indications that the gay and lesbian community might experience similar difficulty with NAP is reported by Sue Hyde of the National Gay and Lesbian Task Force (NGLTF) in Washington D.C. In a May 1988 letter to editors of the gay and lesbian press, Hyde described a 1985 incident when she was falsely led into participation on a panel, purportedly about hate crimes, but which turned out to be "nothing more than a recruitment meeting for the party... I was lied to several times in this whole process." In addition, amongst the panelists was a

Nation of Islam minister who "launched into a very...offensive anti-Semitic, anti-gay diatribe."

— *GAY COMMUNITY NEWS*, OCTOBER 9-15, 1988

We learned right from the start that gay Democrats wouldn't support gay independents, no matter how gay they were. The campaigns run by NAP gay leaders Nomi Azulay, Jim Mangia, Steve Rose and others really exposed the hypocrisy of the official gay leaders and their servility to the Democratic Party. The attacks on NAP in the gay community have been particularly vicious and persistent.

During my 1988 campaign Sue Hyde, the director of the Privacy Project of the National Gay and Lesbian Task Force, went so far as to send a packet of anti-NAP propaganda with a cover letter warning gay leaders of the NAP "menace" to gay media all over the country.

Among other things, she described NAP as being a "cult-like structure under white, male straight party chair Fred Newman." In fact, Emily Carter, an African American woman, was the NAP chair at the time, not Fred. But truth had nothing to do with the attacks on us from the established gay leadership. What the gay Democrats are really concerned about is that they're about to lose their base to independent politics — a base which they need desperately if they are to get patronage jobs with the Democratic Party. I think a lot of the attacks on us really stem from that, not from any principled disagreement with our analysis of what it means to be gay.

When they attempt to give a political or ideological critique of our gay politics, they accuse us of saying that, since people are "only" gay because capitalism is oppressive, once capitalism is done away with no one will be gay any more. What we're actually saying, of course, is that if you do away with capitalism — if you do away with the oppression and repression of this system — *more people* will come out as gay. What will change is that the act of coming out will no longer be an act of political opposition in a society where people are free to live their lives as they see fit, sexually and socially. Right now being gay is an act of rebellion because American society is so homophobic. To misconstrue our position — to turn it on its head — is just disingenuous and opportunistic. It also isn't working. We're building a party that's serious about including the gay community not as tokens but as leaders. That raises real problems for gay Democrats, who regard the gay community as their turf and act (out) accordingly. But people see through it pretty easily.

I want my campaign to be another Stonewall.

> — STEVE ROSE, NAP'S CANDIDATE FOR
> NEW YORK CITY COMPTROLLER IN 1989

By running our gay leaders for office we also established their capacity to provide leadership to *all* people. If you take a look at NAP's history, it becomes very clear that our gay members have been among the major builders and shakers of independent politics. They haven't shrunk from the challenge of going out and organizing all oppressed people.

When NAP went national in the years between 1984 and 1988, many of those who volunteered to leave New York and build the party were lesbians and gay men. In one sense, it would have been easier to send straight men, Black and white, out to build NAP around the country — but that's not what we are. We're about developing leaders from the ranks of the excluded and the despised and the left-out. And the working class has to learn to follow its leaders, whether they're Black or white, gay or straight. We're not interested in having gay tokens; we need gays to lead. That raises all sorts of contradictions and conflicts for people — including the leaders — but we don't back off from those conflicts, we build with them.

I've known Nomi Azulay, our first openly gay candidate, since I met NAP. We've done a lot of campaign work together. She's been willing to go anywhere to build NAP — and has! There's something matter-of-fact about her — she's done the unromantic work of building something out of nothing, and found gratification in that. She's deeply at ease with who she is, and I find that powerful.

Dr. Jessie Fields, a poet as well as a physician, is another one of the people who has worked year in and year out to build NAP. The first time I saw Jessie was at the Castillo Cultural Center, where she was giving a reading of her poetry. She read a poem about daring to not wear earrings. That's always stuck in my mind. We worked together in Chicago and later, in New York City, she became the organizer of my weekly Harlem meetings. It takes a lot for a physician like Jessie to stand on street corners collecting signatures, raising money, doing the unglamorous work of party-building. She has made it clear that she'll do whatever she has to do to help build this movement.

Pam Lewis, the producer of the All Stars Talent Show Network, the largest cultural organization for youth in the country, and I had great fights after she came to New York from Kansas. Learning to engage her nationalism contributed enormously to our growth and development in building NAP. Pam was very young when I first met her; she's grown up with us. We fought our way into an intimate relationship.

Pam comes from a lower-middle-class Black family. She learned her politics in the nationalist, feminist and gay movements on the campus of the University of Kansas at Lawrence, and then she tried to bring those politics to the streets of Harlem and the South Bronx. It raised a lot of conflicts for her. When she first saw the depth of the poverty in the South Bronx, she got sick — literally. She threw up. But she picked herself up and went back to work.

I just love the work she's doing with the All Stars Talent Show Network. As a Black lesbian, she raises all kinds of issues for the young Black men who are working with her — their combination of sexism and homophobia. She's a feisty young woman and I love her dearly.

I've known Jim Mangia for a very long time. He started to work with NAP at about the same time I did. He came out after he joined. He's a good organizer who's probably done more than any single individual to build NAP in California, first in the Bay Area and later in L.A.

Sandra Coleman, the Black lesbian who chairs Minnesota NAP, is delightfully crazy — in the best sense of the word! She embodies so much of who our base is. Her outspokenness and her struggle to overcome her humiliation in order to be here as who she is — which is a powerful leader — represent the best that NAP is. Sandra raises all kinds of problems for some people. They have a hard time with her being so working-class. Sandra is the middle class's worst nightmare — if you give poor people some power, they're going to use it, and use it she does! When I do interviews in Minnesota people say, "Why can't somebody like you be here?" And I say, "Somebody like me *is* in Minnesota."

Harriet Hoffman, the NAP coordinator in the Pacific Northwest, embodies the gutsiness of our Jewish women. Born and brought up on the East Coast, she was willing to pick herself up and go off to Seattle to organize in the Black, gay, Latino, Native American, and white communities so that NAP could be there. That takes a lot of courage. She's been gay-baited and white-baited and cult-baited and she's never backed down. What's so infuriating to me is when Black people there say, "If NAP is Black-led, why is a Jewish lesbian leading it in the Northwest?" Because they ain't building it.

Alvaader Frazier, the founder of the International Peoples' Law Institution, has played a key role in leading and shaping our legal work. Like so many others who came out of the old left, she was abandoned by the old Communist Party. But unlike them she was able to find us and put her revolutionary anger to productive use.

Maria Moschonisiou brings a particular depth to our work, having come out of the European left, the Greek Communist Party, and having a very intimate relationship to the failure of that movement. She had the guts and the smarts to come to the United States and join the most challenging and controversial progressive movement in the world. She played a big role in building the Castillo Cultural Center and getting Fred involved in cultural work.

Steve Rose was a white working-class gay man who worked on my national staff for several years. He died of AIDS late in the spring of 1992.

Steve had been with the Revolutionary Socialist League for many years. He had heard all the rumors about NAP, but he was real and open and decent. So he decided to see for himself. He spent time with us, worked with us, and was moved by what we were doing — actually organizing the working class. It took a lot of guts for him to join NAP.

He tried to introduce us to the left, so that other people could learn what he was learning. But they weren't interested and made him persona non grata. This was very painful to him, because Steve had been a leader on the left — he was very hard working, very likable, and very militant. Once he became associated with NAP — and he was very outspoken about it, as he was about everything else — he went from being a celebrity in the gay and left community to being treated like trash, overnight.

It wasn't Steve's style to apologize for who he was or to hide it — he just sort of barged in with it. He was like that with Reverend Sharpton, with whom he worked for a period of time — very normal and matter-of-fact and completely himself. I think Rev learned a lot from Steve about what it means to be a gay man. Rev liked Steve a lot. They shared a sense of humor, and a willingness to be outrageous.

Among the gay leaders of NAP who have moved me most deeply is Fernando Muñoz, a young working-class Chicano man who died of AIDS in 1990. Fernando's sister, Liz Muñoz, was my vice-presidential running mate in 1992; it was Liz who introduced Fernando to NAP. A very handsome and talented man (he had a degree in filmmaking from Princeton University), Fernando for a long time was too intent on "making it" to realize how high the price of admission is for gay men of color (if you're poor, the price goes up even higher). But ultimately he was too honest and too decent to pretend — to himself, to Liz, or to anyone else — that he could, or wanted, to make it if that meant leaving his people behind (which it did). Fernando Muñoz was a working-class hero — a passionate fighter for what Frantz Fanon called "the wretched of the earth" and defiant in the face of death.

Roslyn Allen, a Black lesbian leader of the Peace and Freedom Party in Northern California, comes out of a political milieu — full of white Democratic Party liberals in the AIDS movement — which is hostile to us. She's weathered a lot of the attacks on us in order to follow the leadership of the New Alliance Party. So many people in California (and everywhere else) know that what we're doing is right on but they don't have the guts to do it with us. They keep silent in the midst of attacks on us instead of defending us and building with us. Roslyn is one of those rare persons who would not keep silent, who stood up for what she knew was right when she could have just as easily shut up and stayed a gay Democrat.

Harold Moore was someone else like that. He was one of my vice presidential running mates in 1988 (I had six, representing various constituencies). He has since died of AIDS. I first met Harold when I went to Oregon as part of our effort to get on the ballot there.

There are two ways to get on the ballot in Oregon: you can collect 35,000 nominating petition signatures, or you can hold a nominating convention by bringing 1,000 registered voters under one roof and getting their signatures. In 1988 we placed an ad in the newspapers inviting people who wanted to help put an independent African American woman presidential candidate (me) on the ballot to give us a call. Many of those who responded were lesbians and gay men who at the time were planning the annual Gay and Lesbian Day parade in Portland. I met with them and we came up with a plan: I would march in the parade, and at the end of the day we would have a rally under a tent — our convention site! (Although several hundred people came, they weren't quite enough to qualify me for the ballot — we ended up having to collect the required 35,000 signatures.)

Harold was assigned to interview me for *Just Out,* a gay magazine in Portland. He started the interview by saying, "I'm a supporter of Michael Dukakis. In 15 minutes convince me to join you."

So I told him who I was, and laid out our campaign plan. At the end of the interview — which lasted an hour and a half — Harold said, "You've got me. What do you want me to do?"

Getting to know him was wonderful. He was decent, open

and very out. While I was on the road he wrote me a letter in which he said that he was a convicted felon and that he had spent time in jail for trying to rob a bank (he hadn't been very good at it). He wanted me to know this, he explained, because when the Dukakis campaign people found out about his past they had distanced themselves from him. He didn't want to embarrass us.

I was very moved and also infuriated — the people who run this country commit major crimes every day of the week, and it never occurs to any of them that *they* might not be good enough. Here was this extremely decent, ordinary human being who felt he had to warn us about himself, who expected us to reject him.

When I went back to Oregon to organize for the convention, I told Harold that he would make a perfect vice presidential candidate — he accepted and he was. He died within a year after the election. I loved him. He was one of those people who touched me and stays with me. He reinforces my sense of why I'm doing what I'm doing.

NAP leaders in general — and you can see that particularly in our lesbian and gay comrades — are gutsy. They'll go places where other people won't tread and do things that other folks won't do. Taking the step to be publicly identified with an organization which is illegitimate is very, very courageous. All of the gay organizers I've been talking about are willing to do some very hard stuff against tremendous odds.

My relationship to the gay community has deepened my humanity. I've learned to say very strongly to Black leaders who are opportunistically homophobic that they can't be anti-gay and pro-Black. Those two perspectives are in complete opposition to each other. One is proclaiming the right to humanity for people and the other is denying someone else's humanity. You can't be on both sides of that issue. You can't be pro-humanity if you're only fighting for a certain element of humanity. If we know the depth of the pain and horror of Black history — a history of be-ing excluded and persecuted and destroyed by virtue of who we are — we should be at the forefront of shaping a movement of inclusion. Homophobia is one of the things that stands in the way of Black people winning the fight for empowerment.

8

HE'S NO GURU, HE'S MY BROTHER

The discipline of psychology did not of course emerge in a social vacuum unrelated to Europe's history of conquest and violence. From its beginning to the present, the discipline has been enmeshed in that history of conquest and violence. This fact is all too often unappreciated and conveniently avoided. Yet for a discipline known for its commitment to unmask the repressed and for its profusion of studies, such neglect and avoidance of human history and the role of psychologists in that history are curious indeed.

— FRANTZ FANON AND THE PSYCHOLOGY OF OPPRESSION,
BY HUSSEIN ABDILAHI BULHAN, 1985

Fred Newman and I first met when Lois Holzman introduced us in 1978. Lois — now an internationally prominent developmental psychologist — and I were colleagues at Rockefeller University, where I was doing work for my doctorate. I went with her to hear Fred speak a couple of times.

At the time I had been in individual therapy with a Black lesbian gestalt therapist for about a year. I wanted to be in group therapy, but my therapist only saw people individually.

I was intrigued when I first came to the New York Institute for Social Therapy and Research. They were talking about therapy and psychology in very progressive ways and they did group therapy, which I found very stimulating intellectually. Social therapy *is* group therapy. The psychotherapeutic task is to build the group as the place where everyone can get help with their emotional problems. Every patient is related to as a revolutionary — that is, as someone capable of reshaping what already exists into something new, despite the fact that all of us have been trained to act out roles in a social play that was written long before we were born. This was fascinating to me. (It still is.)

I chose to be in therapy with Fred because I wanted to work with the top therapist at the Institute, and I knew he was it. At the time, I didn't know much else about him.

The social therapy group I went into was predominantly white and Jewish. (There was one Black man in it.) In the first session I said that there were all these issues I had to work on: I was very angry at Black men; I didn't like white people; and I was in a lot of pain. I wanted to explore all that, and use the group as a context to do some growing. In the beginning it was as if Fred was in the background; over the year my sense of who he was — in the group and in the world — became sharper and sharper.

At the apex of the NAP hierarchy sits Dr. Fred Newman, chief theoretician, campaign manager for Dr. Lenora Fulani, playwright, scholar, activist, and the person who invented the form of therapy practiced by those who have come to be known as the "Newmanites."

— CHIP BERLET, *RADICAL AMERICA*, 1988

The thing that moved me most about being in therapy with Fred was that nothing got covered over — you could talk about anything in that group. It was the first time in my life I ever got to say to white people what I really thought about them — or anything — without getting fired or attacked. I had never experienced — in therapy or in my life — the level of openness that was possible in my social therapy group. And I had a very strong emotional reaction to how supportive Fred was.

I probably spent most of that first year in therapy fighting with the white people in my group. I was used to liberal white people who, when I said things to them about their racism, would be patronizing in response. Then I'd become infuriated and would stop talking to them. But that's not what happened in this group, which was very interesting to me.

I had just separated from my husband, and when I came into group I wanted to talk about all the terrible things that he had done to me that week. One of the women tried to tell me that I was making a big deal out of nothing. It made me so furious. We had a very intense fight. I told the group that they were being disrespectful to me — I sat there and listened to whatever *they* wanted to talk about, all kinds of things that didn't relate to me, that weren't part of my history. Like suicide. At the time I believed suicide was "a white thing," that Black people struggled with life — if we were inclined to be suicidal we would all have killed ourselves when we first experienced racism at the age of five. "To me suicide is white folks' problem," I said. "We aren't the same as you. What I'm saying, whether you like it or not, is that these everyday hassles, trying to deal with my ex-husband and my kids, are what's important to me." Fred supported me. He wasn't condescending. And I began to trust him.

So much was going on in my life during that year. I was thrilled at being free from my marriage, but it was also a very tumultuous time: I was trying to figure out what I was going to do, how I was going to live, who I was going to be.

Then Fred invited me to join the staff of the Institute. I was

very conflicted; I loved social therapy, but I didn't know any-
thing about Marxism, which is what social therapy is based on.
So I invited a group of intellectuals I knew, some of whom were
Marxists, to a meeting with Fred at my house in Brooklyn.
About 40 people came. Except for the people from my social
therapy group who had come, everyone there was Black.

Fred showed up with Phyllis Bolding, a very, very bright,
poor Black woman who was a graduate of the therapist training program and a social therapy patient. (She died a few years
later, probably of a drug overdose.) Phyllis had just come from
a wedding, so she was all dressed up — she was even wearing
white gloves. The middle-class Black people at my house
didn't approve of her at all. She tried to tell them what social
therapy was, but they weren't listening to her. Instead, they
had a four-hour fight with Fred, who fought back. I was
stunned by this whole thing — I had expected that Fred would
come in, talk about social therapy and everyone would love
him like I did.

When I went to group that Friday night I was furious. I
said that the Black people at my house had been trying to tell
them what was going on in the Black community and they
wouldn't listen. Fred said that my friends and colleagues were
being classist, were putting Phyllis down. I refused to hear
him then, mostly because I was so ashamed...I knew he was
right. So that night I fought with my mostly white, mostly
Jewish group about who knew what was best for the Black
community.

When I left, I was very upset. I was about to go to California for a month to look into a job offer I had received from
Michael Cole, for whom Lois and I had worked at Rockefeller
(he had opened the Laboratory of Comparative Human Cogni-
tion there, which later relocated to the University of California

in San Diego), and I didn't want to leave New York on such a sour note.

So I called Fred and made an appointment to have an individual therapy session with him; I wanted to apologize for yelling at everybody, and I wanted to understand what had been going on at my house and in the group. It was a good session. Then I went to San Diego.

I knew two minutes after arriving at the University of California that if I took the job I would spend all my time there fighting — it was so racist. So I turned Mike Cole down and came home to New York in August.

At this point, after I'd been in social therapy for about a year, my gestalt therapist decided to start a group. So I went to my social therapy group and said I was leaving. People tried to reason with me, but I just wouldn't deal with it. I cried through the whole group — it was my way of keeping my distance. As far as I was concerned, there was no choice: an African American woman therapist had formed a therapy group. Period. I was leaving. Fred remained completely silent, while everyone in the group argued with me.

I hated the gestalt group from the beginning. It was everything that social therapy was not: basically individual therapy, just with a lot of people in the room. After two months I called Fred and told him it was the worst experience of my life. He and I went out to dinner a few times. He suggested that I shouldn't leave my new group the same way I had left social therapy, but that I hang in and try to work through my conflicts. I tried, for a few months. Then I came back into social therapy.

Fulani, who has a doctoral degree in developmental psychology, joined Newman's psychotherapy group in the early '80s.

"I organized her," said Newman, Fulani's campaign manager and political mentor. "She is one of my life's proudest accomplishments."

— GEORGE E. JORDAN, *EMERGE*, OCTOBER 1992

During this period in my life, I was going to psychology conferences and fighting with Black psychologists about what I perceived as their racism and their classism toward working-class Black people. I was also writing my dissertation on the anti-poor biases built into the teaching of math to poor children. I went into the public schools to do my research, and found it very hard to be there — to watch children being systematically damaged. That's what Fred and I talked about during these dinners. He didn't tell me that I was "too sensitive" or that I couldn't take everybody's problems to heart, or that I couldn't change the world. That was one of the things I loved about him.

I kept saying we had to do something about what was going on. And I knew that at some point he was going to say, "Okay. Let's do it!" — that I couldn't just keep complaining. That's what these discussions were about — what I was going to do, what kind of psychologist I was going to be, whether I was going to do something that would make a difference. Then he invited me (again) to join the Institute staff. I said that I didn't want to be a token at the Institute — I didn't want to be the only Black person there. So he told me to go out and organize other Black people to come on staff with me.

I pulled together a meeting of about 25 Black women psychologists and invited them to meet with Fred so we could decide whether we wanted to join the staff of the Institute. Among those who joined were Gloria Strickland, who went on to become the director of the Somerset Community Action Program in central

New Jersey, and Emily Carter, who would become my predecessor as the chairperson of the New Alliance Party.

We asked Fred to lead a study group on politics so we could learn more about who he was and who we were. We wanted to read the *Communist Manifesto* with him.

Then my cousin Yvonne's son died. I wanted to give Vonnie everything, because this child had been her heart and soul. But I was panicky, because in the past I had been so easily overwhelmed by what was going on in my family's life that I stopped living my own life. My social therapy group was wonderful. They helped me to define how I could be giving to Vonnie without submerging myself completely in what had happened to her.

I've always felt very passionately about not forgetting Chester and the people I grew up with — especially the people who'd made it possible for me to leave Chester. I feel a very strong obligation to them. Fred taught me a lot about how to give back to Chester without only giving to individuals — which in some ways kept me from giving back to Chester. If I grew, and used who I could be, he said, then I could give them so much more.

That was particularly difficult with my sister Shirley. She's eight years older than I am, and I was crazy about her, as well as very loyal to her; she had been the one adult in my life who wasn't a hypocrite. I had always made it clear to Shirley that I would be with her and for her, in the way she had been for me.

Fred and I did a lot of work on how I couldn't "save" her. (I had worked up a list of about 100 people I was going to go back and rescue.) This work was extremely helpful — it helped me realize I couldn't give to Shirley, or any other individual, in a way that would have made a difference. For one thing, I didn't have very much — materially — myself. Fred was teaching me who I was and who I could be. Poor families — and he knew this from his own experience — only have but so much that they can give. My family had given me everything they had to give. I had gotten it all, and what I needed to do was not to feel guilty, but to figure out how to give it to the world.

The New Alliance Party's "therapy" places an emphasis on overt sexuality and its projects and publications reflect that tone...Several leaders and members have testified to their "love" for Fred Newman. Dr. Lenora Fulani wrote in the National Alliance *(November 16, 1989), "Yes, Fred Newman and I do have a very intimate, close, sensuous, powerful and passionate relationship."*

> — THE NEW ALLIANCE PARTY: A STUDY IN DECEPTION,
> AN ADL RESEARCH REPORT, PUBLISHED BY THE
> ANTI-DEFAMATION LEAGUE OF B'NAI B'RITH, 1990

Fred is probably the only man I had ever met who wasn't out to get something from me. He just gave and gave and gave and gave. It took me a long time to realize that I didn't *have* to give anything back to him. He didn't relate to me as a sexual object. Not that he didn't think I was beautiful and sexy, but that wasn't what our relationship was based on. I wasn't used to it, since I had spent my life learning how to be, and being, a sex object. I think a lot of people who say nasty things about Fred and me just don't get it — they can't imagine how relationships between women and men, between Blacks and Jews, can be organized in a non-exploitative way. When we talk about intimacy, they think we mean fucking.

Fred's never tried to tone me down. He's never patronized me, and he's never agreed with me in order to get me to do something for him, sexually speaking or otherwise.

Thus I would call anti-Semitism a poor man's snobbery. And in fact it would appear that the rich for the most part exploit this passion for their own uses rather than abandon themselves to it — they have better things to do.

— *ANTI-SEMITE AND JEW*, BY JEAN-PAUL SARTRE, 1948

We did a lot of work in my social therapy group on racism. One night a Jewish member of the group started talking about anti-Semitism. There were a lot of Jews in Chester: Jews owned the biggest department store in town; my mother worked for a Jewish family as a domestic; I had many Jewish teachers. I told the group that where I grew up, all white people were the same — we never distinguished between Jews and "other" white people.

That's when I began to learn about anti-Semitism.

Fred told me that when I said that he felt as if I had punched him in the stomach. Now by this time there was no question that I loved this man very dearly. He was opening up possibilities in my life that I never, ever would have even known about. So if he felt that I had attacked him, I took that very, very seriously.

The thing about racism and anti-Semitism is that they're so commonplace. You grow up hearing certain expressions, having certain attitudes, that are so much a part of you that you don't recognize them for what they are. You don't "mean anything" by them. They're so deeply embedded in how you think that they make you insensitive and hurtful even to people you love very much. I worked hard in that group to provide leadership around these issues — to open them up and to deepen them.

Some people in the group had a reaction to me doing this work, and to Fred and me getting closer as a consequence of it. Once one of the men in the group, a Jewish dentist, said some-

thing that was extremely racist. I took him on. But when he
didn't back down, I did. Fred asked me why, and I told him
that I was tired of fighting. Fred said that I had to convey to
Alan that this was my Institute, this was my place, and that if he
wanted to be there he had to conduct himself in acceptable
ways — or else get out.

This wasn't Fred giving me the Institute as my personal
possession. It wasn't that I could wrap it up and take it home
with me. He meant that it was a place where I could be, where
Black people, and Puerto Rican people, and Jewish people, and
working-class people, and gay people — "undesirables" —
could be. It was ours. And that didn't mean that middle-class
people couldn't be there with us — just that they had to be
there on our terms. I had never encountered this anywhere else
in the world. I had spent my whole life looking for this, but had
no idea how to establish these conditions. And here was this
Jewish man I had stumbled upon in my search for a way to express everything I felt about the injustice in the world, and he
was showing me how to do what I had always wanted to do.

*Black families were three times as likely to be poor as White
families. Among Black families maintained by a woman with
no husband present, 52 percent were poor, almost twice the rate
for comparable White families.*

— CURRENT POPULATION REPORTS,
U.S. GOVERNMENT PRINTING OFFICE, MARCH 1988

My father died of a heart attack when I was 12. (We couldn't
get an ambulance to come into our neighborhood.) A week later, my mother's boyfriend, Mr. Smith, came into my life. Mr.
Smith spent the next six years pitting my mother and me

against one another. I vowed I'd never let a man do that to me and my children. Years later, I left my husband Richard because he bullied my children as a way of asserting his manhood. I didn't want to raise them in that kind of environment.

I had Ainka when I was 23, and Amani when I was 27, during the summer that I was studying for my doctoral exams. I used to take Ainka to work with me at Rockefeller University. While we were together Richard and I had "shared" the work of rearing our kids but even then most of it fell on me, as it does on most women. Richard thought of himself as a babysitter. When we separated I had to work, go to school, and take care of two little kids. I've had sole responsibility for them since Amani was one and a half.

When I started becoming involved in NAP in 1981, it was full-time work and very demanding. But it was also a relief from the way I was living my family life. At first Ainka, Amani and I went through some hard times. Once, when I came back from speaking at a convention out of town, Amani had cut clumps of hair out of his head, and Ainka had set the trashcan in our apartment on fire. I sat down and talked with them about the fact that I was becoming very active politically and that it would dramatically change our lives. They needed to decide if they were going to do this with me. We agreed that we would move ahead together.

I formed a child care collective along with Emily Carter, who had a young son, and Luvenia Suber, a NAP organizer, who had a young daughter. We asked Anne Bettman, a founder of NAP who had worked with children for years, if she would be responsible for our kids. Looking back, I think the kids adjusted better to this arrangement than the parents did!

I actually stopped mothering for about six months. I was so relieved that I didn't have the full weight of my children on my shoulders. Then, I started to get involved in their lives again. As they got older, all of us got better at it. I did a lot of work on what they wanted, and if I could give it, I would.

Through all this, I don't think we've ever had a fight which pitted my politics against them. I went on the road during the '88 presidential campaign, and I was out of town for 18 months. Amani and Ainka made a pact not to fight with each other, as a way to support me. I didn't even know about their pact until I came back and, after a few weeks, realized that something was very different!

Without Fred, raising my kids would have been a nightmare. He and I brought them up together. He took on their upbringing in the same way he takes on a political campaign — with the same kind of interest and attention to detail, with the same passion and brilliance. It's been like a work of art. Fred, who's the only man I've let into my children's lives in any real way, knows my relationship with Amani and Ainka better than I do. Thanks largely to him, my kids and I like each other a lot. Every mother should have a Fred Newman in her life.

Both my kids have had very checkered school experiences. When Ainka was in the second or third grade, a private school in Brooklyn called Packer Collegiate Institute accepted her on a full scholarship. And suddenly, she was coming home from school every day crying. This was completely unexpected, because she had always loved public school. So I asked her what was going on. These fancy little WASP kids were calling my daughter "nigger bitch." When I went to speak to the headmaster, he told me that this was a "developmental issue" which Ainka would learn how to handle. I asked him what in the world he was talking about. "This is not a 'developmental issue,'" I said. "This is racism. What are you going to do about it?"

The answer was "nothing."

I talked about what was going on at Packer in my social therapy group. Fred pointed out that I was conveying to Ainka that if she was bright and pleasant and "good" enough she could somehow bypass racism. It came as a big shock to me that I was doing that, and it was an even bigger shock that this Jewish man was pointing it out to me. We did a lot of work on that issue — how *do* you send kids out into a world that's so vicious to them? What tools do you give them? What does it mean that you can't give them the tools to *avoid* something as vicious as racism — that it's not possible?

I started shopping around for another school so I could take Ainka out of Packer as soon as possible. But I was so anxious I couldn't figure out where else to put her. I asked Fred to come with me to an interview with the principal of the Little Red Schoolhouse, an ultra-liberal school in Manhattan where I eventually sent both Ainka and Amani (and from which I soon removed them). I wanted Fred there so he could read the situation and tell me what he thought about it. He took the time to go because he knew how much it meant to me. I told him — jokingly — that if anyone asked me, I would tell them that he was Ainka's father. But they didn't dare ask.

Alarming numbers of left-out teen-agers turn to crime for survival. But their despair should be even more alarming. No society can call itself civilized when so many of its young are being maimed and destroyed so early in life.

— *NEW YORK TIMES*, MARCH 15, 1979

Amani was very young when Richard and I broke up. The combination of who Amani was, or was becoming, and the racism of the liberal middle-class private schools he attended, was very volatile. When he was about three or four years old, his pre-school teacher called to tell me that he was looking under the dresses of the little white girls — that floored me completely. As with most parents of a Black son, everything connected to Amani has a double meaning to me. Mischief is not just mischief; it can so easily be turned into 10 years in reform school, or a label that says, "Destroy this child."

Ainka's always been very personable, very gracious — everybody likes her. She was a social butterfly from the time she was a very little girl. She's every teacher's dream. Amani has always been very rebellious. He was a terror during his brief stay at the Barbara Taylor School, the experimental elementary school in Harlem that I helped to found. Amani was very angry. At the end of the sixth grade he wanted to go to public school and I agreed.

Amani is every teacher's nightmare. He's into the streets, not school. Fred helped teach me that I couldn't control him. I've built my relationship with Amani so that it's open, and not another source of conflict in his life. I tell my children what the streets are like and that they need to make their own decisions about their lives. Amani is a renegade. His teachers get frustrated with him and, I might add, with me. They think he's "wasting" his life, and that I'm being flippant. *He* says he'll come through. I'm going to give him that shot; I'm going to trust him. I think Amani, like many young men, is arrogant. And like so many young Black men, he could end up in serious trouble. When he does something stupid I don't take it personally. I say to him, "That was mighty dumb." I wish he would go to school every day, get As and Bs, do his homework, and stay away from the cops. But that's just not who my son is.

The most traumatic thing about being the mother of a Black male is the cops. Many cops are out to get Black men. That's not paranoia. Amani has had guns drawn on him; he's been arrested. When it's 3 a.m. and he's not home I think he's been murdered. It's a horrendous experience — I hate it. Sometimes I get twinges of guilt, mostly when things aren't going well. I start to think that if I had a nine-to-five job, I could force Amani to study, to go to school. But I know that's ridiculous. I figure out how to work with my real live son Amani rather than succumb to the abstract feelings of guilt that are laid on women.

Fred's brilliance shines through most clearly in my relationship with Amani. I know that because I can see the tension between Amani's friends and their parents.

My fear that something is going to happen to my son, that he isn't going to live, that he's going to be taken away from me — I've not imposed that on Amani, not used it to control him. Fred has helped me to see that if my relationship with Amani expresses anything of the hostility the world directs at him, if I'm trying to get him to do something he doesn't want to do, or can't do, or won't do, that doesn't give him any breathing space. It also doesn't allow our relationship to be useful to him, because I'm just another one of the people in his life who's on his case.

Fred sends Amani to summer camp, and has done that every year for many years. But the most important thing he's done is that he's helped us to create an environment in which Amani can be who he is, and grow, and I can be who I am, and be unoppressive. Amani, Ainka and I have a very decent relationship.

What's so helpful to me is that, when I'm either about to "kill" one of my kids, or I think somebody else is about to kill them, when I know that I can't respond in a way that's going to be productive and useful to them, I've been able to go to Fred and together we figure out what to do.

At one point, Richard wanted to come back into their lives; I was completely opposed to it — he had been really nasty to Amani. Fred and I came up with a great plan. I asked the kids what they wanted to do, and said I would support them, no matter what it was. If I couldn't stand it, I would get the help I needed elsewhere, but they could decide. Ainka wrote him a letter in which she said that she didn't need a father — she needed a friend. Richard probably knew that I was very political, because I've been all over the news, she wrote, but he needed to know that she and Amani were also. They had this great life, there were lots of things they had learned, and they were different people from when he had known them before. So they wanted to talk with him about how he could be in their lives. Richard never responded.

Then Amani decided that he didn't want to see his father until he was 16 or 17, so that if he wanted to get up and walk out, he could.

Things like this, that could have been traumatic, could have turned into a major battle, we handled in ways that were developmental for all of us. Amani and Ainka trust me. They know I speak to Fred all the time about what's going on with them, and I think they feel very comfortable with that.

Fred's there for me and my children — from helping me figure out how to deal with the big things in their lives, to paying for things like summer camp, to dealing with little things that may turn out to be nothing but at the time they're happening seem like major catastrophes. He's always been there for us.

9

PEROT POLITICS

David Frost: When you see the headlines [which say] people shouldn't be able to buy the presidency, what's your answer to that?

Ross Perot: Well, very openly I have said to the American people, "If you want me to I will." And it looks like they want me to. And then the question is, "Who are you buying it for?" I am buying it for them, because I will be their servant. You say, "Well, why don't they buy it for themselves?" They can't afford to.

— "...TALKING WITH DAVID FROST"
PUBLIC BROADCASTING SYSTEM, MARCH 24, 1992

I first heard about Ross Perot from Tom Laughlin, the film actor and director who starred in the *Billy Jack* movies in the early '70s. Laughlin was among a number of progressive insurgents — including Larry Agran and former Minnesota Senator Eugene McCarthy — who ran in the New Hampshire Democratic primary. He put forth a pro-democracy left-populist program that was very compatible with mine. We met at a number of forums during the campaign, and he was always very respectful and supportive of my participation in the election. His supporters walked the picket lines with us at WMUR-TV and outside St. Anselm College, where the two televised debates from which all the insurgents were excluded were held.

Near the end of the New Hampshire primary Laughlin began talking about a Texas billionaire who might make a good candidate if he could be prevailed upon to run. I'd been vaguely aware of Perot before that as the guy who bankrolled all the efforts to find the POWs in Vietnam and who sent his private commandos into Iran to free employees of E.D.S., his computer corporation. But I assumed he was a Republican and didn't think of him as a player in independent politics.

(Laughlin went on to become an activist in the Perot organization, United We Stand, America. On my last trip to California, I heard that he was also planning a new movie project about independent politics.)

I was not at all surprised that 20 to 30 million white people rallied to Perot's banner within a matter of weeks. During my months of campaigning in New Hampshire I'd seen firsthand how hard white working-class and middle-class people there had been hit by the deepening depression. Over and over people told me the most heart-rending stories of lost jobs, foreclosed mortgages, and college educations now out of reach. After four years of hard times, white America wanted a change. Perot wisely thought that such a change might just have to get organized outside the Democratic and Republican parties.

The first direct contact my campaign had with Perot came through John Jay Hooker — a self-described "Kennedy man" who had been the Democratic Party's nominee for governor of Tennessee in 1970 and who had been active in Jesse Jackson's campaign in 1988. Hooker — a good natured and humorous Southern businessman who favors white straw hats and gold pocket watches — played a leading role in convincing Perot to run (the first time) and in convincing him to get back in. In

November of 1991 Hooker had called Perot — at that time they knew each other by reputation only — and asked him to run for president as an independent. When Perot said he wasn't interested, Hooker asked him what he *would* do if he were president. There followed a series of long phone calls throughout December, January and February. The word is that it was Hooker who prevailed upon Larry King to ask Perot about his presidential intentions on the air.

Despite tens of thousands of people calling in their support, Perot was not at all convinced that an independent would be able to get on the ballot in every state. Apparently some of his legal advisers told him that a 50-state run was virtually impossible.

But Hooker was not to be deterred. He contacted the Libertarians' Richard Winger, the pre-eminent ballot-access authority in the country and the editor of *Ballot Access News,* who sent him information on the qualifying requirements and deadlines in every state. Hooker passed the information on to Perot.

Winger also put Hooker in touch with Gary Sinawski, NAP's general counsel, and Jackie Salit, who had helped to coordinate my successful 50-state ballot-access drive in 1988. They met with Hooker in New York at the Regency Hotel and answered scores of questions from the Perot campaign about ballot access. After their meeting, Hooker told a reporter, "Since they [NAP] had done it, it gave me a high level of confidence that it was do-able."

Soon after that, on April 13, I sent the first of a series of letters to Perot, who was still not an announced presidential candidate, but who was racking up signatures on his nominating petitions by the tens of thousands. "Congratulations on scaring the living daylights out of the Washington political establishment!" I wrote. I outlined my work over the last eight years in challenging restrictive ballot-access laws in states around the country and in lobbying for bills on Capitol Hill which would open up the electoral process. I asked him to meet with Fred, who managed both my presidential campaigns, and me. The letter was sent via Hooker, but Perot never answered it directly. Instead, Perot's campaign manager at the time, Tom Luce, a Dallas attorney, called. He said Perot had asked him to speak to me as a prelude to a possible meeting between the two campaigns.

Luce and I spoke directly several days later. Perot and I have yet to meet.

My people continued to meet with Hooker throughout April and May. Meanwhile, I was on the campaign trail; no matter what Perot did, I was going to stay in the race. But I continued to try to influence him. We were urging Perot to reach out in a meaningful way to the African American community, the gay and lesbian community, women and other elements of the Democratic Party's old "New Deal" coalition. We pointed out that he had already drawn the bulk of the Republican voter support that would come his way and that if he wanted to put together a majoritarian base which could erode Clinton's support as well as Bush's and actually win the election, he would have to include the African American electorate. On May 29, at the Hotel Carlyle in New York we conveyed this political message to Hooker, who in turn would report to Perot. It turned out though, that several hours earlier the *New York Post* had "broken" the story that Perot had told Barbara Walters in an exclusive interview for ABC-TV's "20/20" that he wouldn't appoint any gay people to high-level Cabinet posts.

That day at the Carlyle, Hooker was extremely agitated and the Perot campaign was in an uproar. Hooker had been getting calls all day from political types around the country who were sure Perot had fatally wounded himself. Hooker said he had spoken with Jackie Jackson, Jesse Jackson's wife (and supposedly a closet Perot supporter), who was very upset. Hooker had been trying to reach Perot all day, unsuccessfully. He, too, was worried that the gaffe would be very costly, and was pacing the floor of the hotel suite, fielding calls and muttering about how Perot should go to Europe for the summer so he wouldn't say anything else damaging.

My people tried to calm him down. We told him that Perot's comments seemed more indicative of his recognition of the homophobia that pervades America, which would generate a lack of confidence in gay appointees, than his own anti-gay bias. We also told him that it was Democratic Party gay leaders, who were anti-Perot and desperate for a Clinton victory, who were bent on sensationalizing the story. We counseled that it was now more important than ever for Perot to reach out to disenfranchised constituencies, and lobbied for a meeting between Perot and me. Hooker agreed to pursue it.

In the meantime Debra Olson, a California-based lesbian activist in the Perot movement, whom I would later come to know, respect and love, was pressing Perot to meet with a group of lesbian and gay leaders from around the country. She ultimately pulled off the meeting and became Perot's leading adviser on lesbian and gay issues. Olson told me that — after the meeting with Perot, his wife Margot and Perot's campaign adviser, Mort Meyerson, — she was so impressed with Ross' openness that she jumped into the campaign "with both feet." She convinced Perot that he needed to issue a statement clarifying his position on lesbian and gay issues, and told me months later that the fact that this "old school Texas boy" (as she put it) used the term "sexual orientation" showed her that he wasn't interested in playing only to his politically conservative followers.

I believe it would be disruptive for us to continue our program
since this program would obviously put [the election] in the
House of Representatives and be disruptive to the country.

— ROSS PEROT, ANNOUNCING THAT HE WAS DROPPING OUT OF
THE PRESIDENTIAL CAMPAIGN, JULY 16, 1992

On the morning of Thursday, July 16 — the fourth and final day
of the Democratic National Convention in New York and the day
that Clinton was set to accept his party's nomination — Perot
called a press conference and declined the nomination of the 30
million Americans who supported his independent candidacy.

"Frankly, it couldn't happen at a better moment," said
George Stephanopoulos, Clinton's communications director.
With Perot out of the race, Clinton, who a month earlier had
been coming in third behind Perot and Bush in the polls,
weighed in with a 23% lead over the former president. He never
lost the lead again.

While I had been urging Perot to meet with me and the
other independents, he apparently had been talking instead to
the Democrats. I don't know for sure what went down, but I
do know that he was in New York for an unannounced and
undisclosed "private meeting" early in the week of the
Democratic Party convention. I do know that Jesse Jackson,
who had met with Perot during the last week in May, and who
could have taken his base independent with Perot and helped
him win the White House, stayed put in the Democratic Party
and that by mid-week Perot had pulled out with a rather shocking statement that described the Democratic Party as "revital-
ized" — he said it four times in the course of the short announcement!

Perot has since given a number of explanations for his withdrawal — from his fears of destabilizing the electoral process to Republican plans to disrupt his daughter's wedding. But in June, with his popularity slipping under a barrage of vicious attacks from the Republicans (and more covertly from the Democrats) Perot did what any good businessman would do — he cut his losses.

Of course, the deal did not go down well with his followers. Perot was once again flooded with telegrams, letters and phone calls, this time demanding that he hang in there. Hooker called and said that he was already in the midst of convincing Perot to get back in the race. One telegram I read sticks in my mind. It was from Bob Hayden, chairman of the California Perot Petition Committee, and it read in part, "We, your millions of supporters, respectfully decline to accept your statement and we demand your presence in the White House. We are deeply committed to your candidacy and we are not going away."

And they didn't.

Over the weekend of July 17, the 50 state coordinators descended on Dallas to demand that Perot re-enter the race. Although Perot, at that time, resisted their pleas, the state coordinators vowed to finish the job of putting him on the ballot in every state — which, of course, they did.

Cathy Stewart, who later became my chief of staff, was in Dallas that weekend talking to the Perot leaders about the need to hook up with the rest of the independent movement and distributing my position paper entitled, *How the Populist Supporters of Ross Perot and the Democrats' "New Deal" Center-Left Coalition Can Use the 1992 Presidential Election to Build a Majoritarian New Democracy Alliance, Win the White House in 1996 and Rebuild America in the 21st Century — A Black and White Paper,* which urged Perot's supporters to remain independent and find a way to work with the African American and other minority communities.

In subsequent weeks the paper was fedexed, faxed, mailed, xeroxed, borrowed, reprinted, quoted and read aloud by independent political activists around the country. Perot supporters forwarded it to the once and future candidate with personal cover letters beseeching him to heed the advice inside. African American followers of Jesse Jackson tried to put copies in Jackson's hands in a last ditch effort to win him over to the strategy I put out in the paper — that the only viable plan for Black empowerment was for the Rainbow to break with the Democratic Party and join with the Perot base.

In the *Black and White Paper* I wrote:

> An alliance of these two grassroots camps — the independent center-left Rainbow and the radical populist center — would create a new electoral majority that could overtake the center-right Democrats and Republicans in four years. To create this alliance, a substantial portion of the Perot base must stay independent in 1992. A substantial portion of the Black-led multi-racial wing of the working-class independent movement must vote independent in 1992...If the Fulani base and the Perot base combine in a new democracy alliance, there will be enough votes to guarantee a victory in 1996, no matter what the outcome of 1992.

From then on an important part of my campaign became the work of building ties with the newly emerged independents. When NAP held its national convention over the weekend of August 22-23, we invited all the pro-democracy independent parties and organizations to send a representative and participate in a panel called "Independent Politics: the Shape of Things to

That's me at the piano. My young admirer is my sister Lolita's son Robert, whose nickname was "Buby." He and his brother were two of my favorites.

I was about 14 when this school picture was taken.

Senior prom night, 1968. The laughing young woman next to me was one of my best friends, Jill Council. Tragically, Jill died a few years ago. ▶

(Facing page) From my freshman year — in the Rathskeller at Hofstra University. 1968.

My maternal grandparents, Frank and Priscilla Stack. ▶

The younger generation at my grandparent's 50th wedding anniversary celebration. My brother Roosevelt is seated at the right and my mother is seated at the left. Standing in the first row, from left to right: Nora (a family friend), my cousins Yvonne (Vonnie), Arnita and Barbara (Bob), my sister Delores and me. Left to right in the back row: My cousins Bootsie and Jerome, and my sisters Shirley and Lolita. Arnita, Bootsie and Lolita have all died since this picture was taken.
▼

My kids, Ainka and Amani Fulani — they're beautiful, aren't they?

I gave this picture to my mother. The note I wrote on the back said, "To Mom, from your beautiful Black daughter (smile). Love, Lenny." ▲

Amani and Ainka after her appearance in a dance recital. ▶

With my children at NAP's 1992 presidential nominating convention. ▼

(Facing page) My mother, Pearl Branch, and me outside my sister's house in Chester, Pennsylvania. My mother was 76 years old when this picture was taken in 1991.

"I'm your sexual preference!" Gay Pride March '92, New York City. Rap artist M.C. Browneyes is on the microphone.

On vacation in Jamaica in 1980 with Gloria Strickland, who has been my friend since we were undergraduates at Hofstra. She is the executive director of the Somerset (New Jersey) Community Action Program and a leader of the New Alliance Party.

In June 1987 I traveled to Cuba to attend the biennial gathering of the Interamerican Congress of Psychology. One of my most moving experiences was the chance to meet the Cuban people, including this family in Havana.

▲ At a conference entitled "Prospects for Democracy in Zaire" held in Washington, DC on November 16, 1990. Standing next to me is Dr. Georges Nzongola-Ntalaja, a professor of African Studies at Howard University and , later, a delegate to the Sovereign National Conference 1991-1992 in Kinshasa. Next to him is Nancy Ross, the executive director of the Rainbow Lobby. To her left is Etienne Tshisekedi wa Mulumba, who later became the prime minister of Zaire.

On the democracy picket line outside the presidential debate in Manchester, New Hampshire in February 1992 with members of the All Stars Talent Show Network. Music producer Tony Rose is at left. ◀

Following the Rodney King verdict, I addressed a rally at Columbia University in New York City. May 1992. ▶

"End AIDS Now! No Justice, No Peace!" I take time out from NAP's nominating convention to lead a march on the New York City campaign headquarters of George Bush and Bill Clinton. August 23, 1992.

Come." Those who came were: Norma Segal, the Libertarian Party candidate for U.S. Senate from New York; Dr. John Hagelin, the presidential candidate of the Natural Law Party; and John Atkisson, of United We Stand, America in Oklahoma.

Representatives of the Libertarians, United We Stand and Natural Law also attended a number of NAP state conventions in September. At the same time, United We Stand invited representatives of NAP and my campaign to attend a number of their meetings in California, Indiana and Minnesota. Natural Law went out of its way to include me and the New Alliance Party in events in which they were participating.

The Libertarian Party — which has been around since 1973 and advocates a sort of idealized version of 19th century "free enterprise" capitalism — kept its distance in 1992 from both NAP and the newly emerging independent forces. The party's presidential candidate, Andre Marrou, shunned coalitional work and pursued a strategy of projecting the Libertarians as *the* independent party.

On October 30, I debated Marrou one-on-one on C-Span. I had pushed for the inclusion of Hagelin and other independents, but only NAP and the Libertarians met C-Span's criterion of being on the ballot in enough states to have a mathematical chance of winning the Electoral College. Marrou used the opportunity to push his party, and I used it to urge the viewers to vote independent — which reflected our two differing approaches to the election.

However, at the same time that Marrou was distancing himself, other prominent Libertarians continued to be friendly to NAP and the other independents. Rich Winger — who is unremittingly principled and helpful to all independents regardless of their ideology — sent a telegram to the NAP convention which read, "The thing I love most about the New Alliance

Party is its eagerness to work with everybody that agrees with it about democracy."

During the period when Perot was out of the race, a number of important leaders and organizations — serious about building independent politics and open to working with the Black community — emerged.

One of the most important, and someone to whom I feel personally very close, is Debra Olson, the chairperson of the California Civil Rights Committee of United We Stand. Debra is the granddaughter of Culbert Olson, the first Democratic governor of California, and the daughter of a judge. She entered politics as a volunteer in April of 1992 and was soon involved in some major projects for Perot, acting as his national liaison to the lesbian and gay community.

When Perot dropped out in June, Debra not only pressured him to return, but began to look around for alternatives.

She heard about me through John Hagelin, a Harvard-educated physicist who teaches at Maharishi International University in Fairfield, Iowa. He is among the 4,000 people who this April (just as Olson was joining the Perot campaign) got together in Fairfield to form the Natural Law Party.

The Natural Law Party, springing initially from the community of people who practice transcendental meditation, had in six short months garnered support from a wide cross section of the American people — earning federal primary matching funds, getting Hagelin on the ballot in 29 states and fielding 125 candidates in 32 states — a tribute both to their hard work and the hunger of the American people for an alternative to the two-party system. On October 23, Natural Law broadcast a 30-minute "advertorial" on NBC-TV. The party received 30,000 calls in response to the broadcast — three times as many as Perot received after his first half-hour ad — and raised half a million dollars, enough to buy another 30 minutes of time.

The New Alliance Party has been perhaps the most open [of the independent forces] in recognizing the value of our party and our ideas, and that's very welcome. The purpose of our party is not to create career politicians but to bring solutions that work. Lenora Fulani has been very open herself to that type of thinking and that type of approach.

— JOHN HAGELIN, QUOTED IN THE
NATIONAL ALLIANCE, NOVEMBER 5, 1992

One of the ways NAP and Natural Law wound up cooperating in '92 was by running joint candidates for office. In the state of Vermont our gubernatorial candidate ran on a combined ticket of the Natural Law and New Alliance parties. We also cross-endorsed candidates in districts where one or the other of us didn't have a candidate of our own. That kind of non-sectarian cooperation is very important — and very new. It establishes a model that I think will serve us well in the future.

After Perot dropped out, Debra Olson went to Iowa to check out the Natural Law Party. She heard a lot of talk about me and the work Natural Law was doing with NAP. She was intrigued by the fact that a Black woman was running for president, so she called my office and pretty soon we were talking frequently. She attended the California NAP convention and soon after that I invited her — along with John Hagelin and representatives of the Libertarians — to come to New York to discuss what work we could do together before the election.

At that meeting we agreed to work together to push for open debates which would include all significant independents.

We also drafted what would turn out to be our last letter to Perot before the election. We called for a meeting to discuss common issues facing the independent movement:

> We propose a private meeting with you to discuss possible joint ventures aimed at a radical deregulation of two-party monopoly politics in America. For example, one cutting edge issue at this time is presidential debates — whether they will be held at all, and if they are, whether the Democrats and Republicans will once again get away with excluding significant independent candidates...

> The debate is but one example. There is much for us to talk about. The signers of this letter represent organizations of diverse — and growing — constituencies. The Libertarian Party, on whose ticket Andre Marrou is running for president, is fielding over a thousand candidates for local office. The Natural Law Party represents a newly politicized base of $2\frac{1}{2}$ million followers. The New Alliance Party and Dr. Fulani have a substantial base nationally among African Americans, Puerto Ricans and Chicanos, as well as among progressive whites. United We Stand, America, as you know, continues to speak on behalf of millions of Americans disaffected with the political system. We believe the time is right for a dialogue with you.

It was signed by John Hagelin, Debra Olson and me, as well as Steve Givot, secretary of the Marrou campaign, and Linda Pittman, a member of the California State Steering Committee of United We Stand. Debra delivered the letter. A week later Perot re-entered the race.

I know I hurt many of the volunteers who worked so hard through the spring and summer when I stepped aside in July. I thought it was the right thing to do. I thought that both political parties would address the problems that face the nation. We gave them a chance. They didn't do it. But the volunteers on their own forged ahead and put me on the ballot in the final 26 states after July 16. The day we were on the ballot in all 50 states the volunteers requested that I come back in because the political parties had not responded to their concerns...There's only one issue now, starting today, and that is what's good for our country.

— ROSS PEROT, ANNOUNCING HIS DECISION TO
RE-ENTER THE RACE FOR PRESIDENT, OCTOBER 1, 1992

There is absolutely no doubt in my mind that the reason Perot re-entered the race was because the "volunteers," as he calls his supporters, just wouldn't quit. They put him on the ballot in all 50 states, even when he said he wasn't a candidate, they kept their state and local organizations in place, they held conferences, and they reached out to other independent forces.

There was no guarantee they would stick around. What the United We Stand folks did was, in fact, unprecedented. They built and sustained a movement without a leader and forced Perot — despite whatever deal he had cut with Clinton — back into the race. The United We Stand folks have what it takes to build a movement.

I was tickled pink to see Ross up there debating Clinton and Bush. Not only did he win the debates in terms of making the most sense, we *all* won because an independent was up there. We had worked long and hard to see that happen.

There's no way the Commission on Presidential Debates or the League of Women Voters, or whoever or whatever winds up sponsoring presidential debates in 1996, can keep significant independents out again. I guarantee you there will never be another presidential debate that includes only a Democrat and a Republican. From now on, it will be three, maybe four candidates who will put their views before the American people. Independent politics has established that it will be included.

There are many different forces now participating in the independent political movement, all potential partners in what could evolve into a major coalitional third party that is genuinely democratic, multi-racial and multi-constituency — and one that could command a sufficient plurality to win the White House in 1996.

The 21st Century Party, chaired by United Farm Workers co-founder Dolores Huerta, was founded by leaders of the National Organization for Women and the Fund for a Feminist Majority, entities which already have an extensive base and organizational structure throughout the country. The origins of 21st Century go back to 1988, when rank-and-file members of NOW raised questions about the organization's lopsided marriage to the Democratic Party (the women gave everything and the Democrats gave nothing) and wondered why I — as the only woman in the race — had been excluded from addressing a number of NOW events. Molly Yard, at that time the president of the organization, told the press that year, "In terms of a person like Ms. Fulani, we are basically not interested in a third party candidacy, because the experience in this country on third party candidates is that it's a lost cause."

But the rank and file's interest in independent politics was strong enough that at the '89 convention it voted to establish the Commission for a Responsible Democracy. When it finally completed its "investigation" three years later and reported back to the ranks at NOW's 1992 convention, the membership voted overwhelmingly to support the formation of a new party. It was too late to participate in the '92 elections, but it has been founded!

I want to congratulate the New Alliance Party on their pioneering work making the ballot more accessible to voters, so that voters can have alternative choices.

— DOLORES HUERTA, IN A TELEGRAM
TO THE NAP CONVENTION, AUGUST 22, 1992

The week after the NAP convention I attended the founding convention of the 21st Century Party in Washington, DC. Dolores Huerta has since taken part in a number of discussions with NAP, Natural Law and United We Stand about possible joint work.

However, the leadership of NOW continues to keep one foot in the Democratic Party. With a Democrat in the White House and more women Democrats having been elected to office in 1992, it remains to be seen if the 21st Century Party develops into a real independent force. They're going to keep a close eye on the Clinton administration to see how things unfold. It's up to the rank and file of the organization to continue to push the need to leverage a feminist agenda through independent politics, and I wish the sisters all the courage and determination they're going to need.

Whatever the outcome of this year's Presidential race, historians will undoubtedly focus on 1992 as the beginning of the end of America's two-party system.

— THEODORE LOWI, *NEW YORK TIMES SUNDAY MAGAZINE*,
AUGUST 23, 1992

The Independence Party was formed in September of 1992 by Lowell Weicker, the independent governor of Connecticut; former Senator John Anderson, who split from the Republican Party in 1980 when Ronald Reagan won the nomination and ran for president as an independent that year, winning six million votes; and Theodore Lowi, the John L. Senior Professor of American Institutions at Cornell University who, together with pollster Gordon Black, conducted a poll in the spring of 1992 which showed that 60% of the American people favored the establishment of a new political party.

In October I met with Governor Weicker, a former U.S. senator and liberal Republican who was elected as the candidate of the independent "A Connecticut Party." I found him to be a very congenial and straightforward man. He wanted to know how NAP had managed to get me on the ballot in all 50 states in 1988, how we raised money, the details of ballot-access restrictions around the country — nuts and bolts stuff. He modestly pointed out that his A Connecticut Party had only succeeded in electing him and his lieutenant governor in one small state. He also emphasized his belief that the new independent party must be built around "centrist" issues which he defined as the economy, health care and an urban agenda.

I told him that I thought it was the democracy issue which tied all of these other issues together. We also discussed the African American community and my role as the link between Black people and the broader independent movement. My impression was that Governor Weicker was very respectful of that.

MANCHESTER, N.H.—Lenora B. Fulani looks just like a major Democratic candidate. She has received more matching federal campaign funds than Paul Tsongas and Jerry Brown.

She dashes about the state in rented cars, surrounded by frantic aides. She even earned a standing ovation from the New Hampshire Junior Women's Club.

Not bad for a Marxist candidate.

While Marxism has died in most of the world, Fulani and her New Alliance Party have emerged as the nation's only thriving left-wing party.

— *USA TODAY*, FEBRUARY 17, 1992

What I have in common with Ross Perot and Al Sharpton and Lowell Weicker and John Hagelin and Debra Olson and even Andre Marrou and the Libertarians is that we are all convinced that matters must be put (or put back) into the hands of the American people. Democracy as a two-party monopoly isn't working for the majority of us. It's dead. It needs to be buried. Democracy that is a sham consensus supporting a ruling elite isn't a democracy for the 21st century. Democracy must be opened up, deregulated, radicalized.

Democracy means rebuilding America — making it productive again without doing so on anybody's back. Al Sharpton and Debra Olson and John Hagelin are very decent and wonderful people who have their own views and their own ideas and I respect them. What we all share is a humanism for a new century. Together we can contribute to building a new America.

10

SUPPORTING
PEOPLE'S STRUGGLES
THE WORLD OVER

The Caribbean is now an American sea...Trujillo gone, Duvalier of Haiti is the uncrowned king of Latin American barbarism. It is widely believed that despite the corruption and impertinence of his régime, it is American support which keeps him in power: better Duvalier than another Castro.

— C.L.R. JAMES IN HIS APPENDIX TO
*THE BLACK JACOBINS: TOUSSAINT L'OUVERTURE
AND THE SAN DOMINGO REVOLUTION*, 1962

In January of 1987, one year after the overthrow of Jean-Claude "Baby Doc" Duvalier, Papa Doc's equally hated son, I went to Haiti for the first time. The peasant-based Congress of Democratic Movements — its Kréyole acronym is KONAKOM — had invited me, through the Rainbow Lobby, to attend a national dialogue on democracy. The slogan of the conference was "Tet Ansanm Pou Sa Chanje" ("Heads Together for This Change"). Except for some representatives from a U.S. Quaker organization, there were very few Americans at the conference.

The conference was called to discuss the newly proposed Haitian constitution, which was later adopted in a national referendum that set Haiti on a rocky road to democracy and self-determination. More than 1,000 people from all over the country poured into a Salesian retreat outside the Haitian capital, Port-au-Prince, where the conference was held. The heated debate covered everything from the new constitution to agricultural concerns and problems in breeding pigs. It was very raucous. And while I didn't speak a word of French or Kréyole, nor did I know the first thing about farming or livestock, I felt very much at home there.

I made a brief unity statement at the conference expressing our support for the struggle for democracy in Haiti. Michael Hardy, who made the trip with me, and I met numerous Haitian leaders at the conference, among them Victor Benoit, a leader of KONAKOM (I would later come to know him much better), and Robert Duval, who worked on behalf of political prisoners. In between conference sessions we walked the streets of Port-au-Prince and shook people's hands. We spent several days there, and made some friends.

What struck me most about Haiti was the overwhelming poverty, and the presence of the military everywhere. Duvalier was gone, but the dreaded Tonton Macoutes, his paramilitary enforcers, still terrorized the country with the tacit permission of the government of Lt. General Henri Namphy, who took power after the overthrow of Baby Doc. The suffering was so acute. If you had any compassion as a human being, your immediate impulse was to roll up your sleeves and start doing something about it right away.

I saw nearly naked people out in the street going through bags of clothing donated by some charitable organization, looking for something they could wear. It was so painful and upsetting; Haiti is practically next door to the United States, and this is the 20th century, but Haiti looked like a scene from the Middle Ages.

One night while we were there a woman was murdered in the street not too far from our hotel, the Holiday Inn in Port-au-Prince. The army just left her body there, as a warning to others; there were constant tensions between soldiers and the people, and scuffles were always breaking out.

Going to Haiti was an invaluable experience; having seen and experienced the injustice there firsthand brought me very close to the struggle of the Haitian people. I feel part of that struggle, obligated to it.

That trip began the process, which continued throughout 1987, of my breaking out of my parochialism and expanding my horizons as a leader. (I had never been out of the country before except for a vacation I took to Jamaica with my old friend Gloria Strickland after I ended my marriage.) This was my first practical lesson in U.S. foreign policy. It had a huge impact on me. Little did I know that this trip would later lead to my being right in the middle of both the tidal wave of democratic revolt that elected Father Jean-Bertrand Aristide to the presidency, and the treachery which sold him out.

We have no reason to not take the CNG [the provisional government established after the overthrow of Duvalier — LBF] at their word that they are committed to elections and democracy.

— A REAGAN STATE DEPARTMENT SPOKESPERSON ON THE EVE
OF HAITI'S FIRST SCHEDULED ELECTION IN NOVEMBER 1987

It would be as if Hitler had left Germany, and Goebbels, Himmler and Goering were left to conduct "free elections."

—BEN DUPUY, EDITOR OF *HAITI PROGRES*,
COMMENTING ON THE SAME SITUATION, OCTOBER 1987

But before all of that would unfold, the elections scheduled for

November 29, 1987 were drowned in blood, with dozens of Haitian voters slaughtered by the Macoutes and the military as they stood on line at the polls. Despite escalating official violence in the weeks prior to the election — including the murder of two presidential candidates and the burning down of the headquarters of the independent Provisional Electoral Council (CEP) — in the weeks before the slaughter, liberals in Congress (including Congressional Black Caucus members) who had been monitoring the election process were suddenly quiet. Among them was Congressman Walter Fauntroy of the District of Columbia, the chair of the Congressional Task Force on Haiti, who joined the Reagan administration in looking the other way. Fauntroy and Senator Bob Graham of Florida went on a "fact-finding" trip prior to the scheduled election; on their return, a spokesperson claimed that "the violence was not systemic, not part of a military policy." A Fauntroy staffer said at the time that he felt the Reagan administration was working "quietly but effectively" to support free elections. When the bloodbath took place on the day of the election (which was canceled midway through the day), I publicly charged Fauntroy and other Democrats who stood by with being responsible. They supported the U.S. State Department policy that destroyed democracy in Haiti at its birth.

The election day killings forced Washington to cut off military aid to Namphy's National Governing Council (CNG), although the State Department recognized the CNG-run election of January 1988 in which Leslie Manigat became the new president. (The election had been boycotted by all the major candidates.) Despite the aid cutoff, repression against the democracy movement intensified, and in June of 1988 Namphy staged a coup which returned him to power. In September, in the midst of a wave of strikes and demonstrations, Namphy was overthrown in another coup by pro-democracy members of the military, and a former Duvalier adviser, Lt. General Prosper Avril, seized power, promising new elections in 1990.

On the streets and in the countryside of Haiti, one atrocity after another was being committed by the Macoutes. Avril and his cronies — with silent support from the State Department and the U.S. Embassy — gave the Macoutes license to repress any democratic impulse on the part of the Haitian people. The Haitian community was rife with stories of people being dismembered by the Macoutes; it was awful, everyone's worst nightmare. I took part in almost all the demonstrations in the U.S. that were held to protest the brutality of the regime and its strangling of the democratic process. But despite the repression, popular resistance continued to swell. Amid a new wave of strikes and demonstrations, Avril boarded one of the seemingly regular flights carrying unpopular Haitian rulers to safety in the United States; pending new elections Ertha Pascal-Trouillot, the only woman on Haiti's Supreme Court, was sworn in as interim president.

In the sermon-like speeches that antagonized his enemies and mesmerized his followers, Father Jean-Bertrand Aristide often described his movement as a **lavalas,** *the Haitian term for a cleansing avalanche that will wash away tyranny and corruption. That image was particularly relevant last week, as a political* **lavalas** *carried the 37-year-old Roman Catholic priest to an overwhelming victory in Haiti's first truly democratic presidential elections.*

— *TIME,* DECEMBER 31, 1990

In the summer of 1990, I got a call from Judy Jorrisch, a NAP member and friend who had been contacted by Lionel Derenoncourt, an old friend of hers, about the situation in

Haiti. A U.S.-based ally of KONAKOM, Lionel wanted to set up a meeting with Victor Benoit, whom I had met briefly in Haiti in 1987, and Fred and myself. Of course we agreed.

Benoit, Derenoncourt, Fred and I met at Fred's therapy office on West 72nd Street in Manhattan. Benoit and I shook hands, remembering our first meeting in Haiti three years earlier. The leader of the largest peasant organization in the country, he was nevertheless very unassuming. I was drawn to him. He talked with us about the situation in Haiti and the upcoming national elections, scheduled for November 4. Ertha Pascal-Trouillot was interim president at that point, and things had become relatively stable, at least for the moment. Benoit told us of a broad coalition of left-of-center forces which had come together under the name National Front for Democracy and Change — FNCD. The FNCD was planning a convention at which it would nominate its presidential candidate. Benoit explained that as the left-of-center candidate with a mass base, he was the likely choice of the FNCD. The U.S. State Department was backing a former World Bank official — Marc Bazin.

Benoit and Derenoncourt asked us to lobby on Capitol Hill for the U.S. to strengthen the security situation surrounding the forthcoming election.

Benoit also wanted our support to help thousands of local candidates — many of them KONAKOM activists — run for office on the FNCD ticket. Money was needed to fund their registration fees, and Fred and I quickly agreed that we would mobilize our networks to come up with the funds. Several days later, when Benoit left the U.S. to return to Haiti, we had raised $10,000 for the effort. Several weeks later, through the Rainbow Lobby and NAP, we put together another $10,000 and wired it to KONAKOM. The FNCD campaign was underway and the prospects for an election that would sweep thousands of pro-democracy activists into local and national office looked promising — until the Duvalierists struck back. In July, two of the most hated and feared Duvalierists — Roger Lafontant, the chief of the Tonton Macoutes under Papa and Baby Doc, and Williams Regala, the Duvalier thug who orchestrated the November 1987 election day massacre — returned to Haiti. Arrest warrants were issued for these fascists, but Pascal-Trouillot was powerless to execute any of them. KONAKOM led a one-day general strike, temporarily foiling plans for a right-wing coup, and then Victor Benoit turned to me for help. I contacted the Rainbow Lobby, asking Nancy Ross, the executive director, and Deborah Green, the Lobby's political director, to put together an emergency conference on Capitol Hill, which they and their staff did on just four days' notice. On July 20 dozens of Caribbean activists, congressional staffers, human rights workers, church people, lawyers and journalists packed a room in the Senate Russell Office Building that Ted Kennedy's office made available.

On a telephone hookup from Haiti, KONAKOM leader Jean-Claude Bajeux, a Harvard-educated former Jesuit priest who was exiled by Papa Doc in 1964 for his political activity (his family was also murdered), addressed the conference. While Benoit had developed as a grassroots leader of the impoverished Haitian peasantry (which makes up over 90% of the country), Bajeux was an international human rights activist who had developed connections within both the international socialist movement (the Second International) and the U.S. State Department. Bajeux gave a detailed briefing on the political situation inside the country. He also appealed for us to put pressure on Jimmy Carter, who as chairperson of the Council of Freely Elected Heads of Government was once again getting involved in the Haitian electoral picture (as he had prior to the bloodbath of 1987). Following the conference, we began to pressure Carter not to go to Haiti and to issue a public call for Lafontant's arrest.

Though the Capitol Hill briefing was very successful, a strain soon became apparent in my relationship with Victor. He began to ask that I soft-pedal my support for him and the FNCD. It seemed that Bajeux was counseling him not to become overidentified with me, NAP or the Rainbow Lobby. Victor insisted that it was "nothing personal"; the interests of KONAKOM and the Haitian struggle were best served by the broadest possible coalition of support. I agreed. The more the better, I told him. But there was just one problem. No one in the United States, on *his* account, was doing anything to help them, except for us. But even so, I agreed to Victor's request and we stopped publicizing his cause to give him room to attract other supporters.

In the meantime, though, two important developments were taking place behind the scenes. One, there was factional strife inside the FNCD. The nominating convention was postponed. It was not clear whether Victor was going to get the presidential nomination.

At the same time, the State Department had gone to work. Though the U.S. was officially supporting the pro-Washington, DC Marc Bazin, the State Department, the CIA, etc., were smart enough to realize that Bazin was not hugely popular and that the left-of-center FNCD candidate might actually win in a fair election. Thus the State Department was motivated to maintain good relations with Benoit. Bajeux served as the go-between in that relationship, and soon began to lobby Benoit on behalf of the American ambassador, Alvin Adams, and his political officer, Robert Holly, with whom Bajeux was in frequent contact.

Holly did not want Benoit to have anything to do with me. It was that simple. I believe that Bajeux was told that a continued alliance with me would mean that Benoit would forfeit any protection and legitimization that the U.S. Embassy had to offer. After all, the Macoutes were still operating and Benoit's life was in danger. He slept at a different house every night for security reasons. The embassy did have the capacity, though, to exert "friendly persuasion" on the Macoutes and get them to leave Victor be. Holly was playing hardball: Break with NAP or lose our support.

Meanwhile, the Rainbow Lobby had been working to organize a national tour for Benoit in this country; no doubt the many phone calls Nancy Ross was making to arrange speaking engagements for him exacerbated the antagonism of Holly's bosses in the State Department toward Victor Benoit's "dangerous liaisons" with us.

Holly called the shots; Bajeux, who did the dirty work, began making it clear that the "romance" was over. NAP and the Rainbow Lobby decided that a meeting was necessary to clear the air. It was scheduled for October 16, when Bajeux and Benoit would be in New York City to attend a meeting of the Second International, the worldwide coalition of socialist governments and movements. The night of the meeting, Bajeux called Jackie Salit — who was representing me, since I was out of town — to say that they were very pressed for time. He asked her to come by a party at the headquarters of Local 1199 to talk; clearly he wanted to avoid any kind of serious discussion. Jackie refused, suggesting instead that Bajeux and Benoit come to the Rainbow Lobby's "hospitality suite" at the Waldorf-Astoria Hotel, where the Second International meeting was taking place. Reluctantly, he agreed.

The meeting, which Jackie, Fred, Deborah Green and

Gabrielle Kurlander, Fred's special assistant, attended, was fairly brief and had its comic moments: someone kept knocking on the door to say that the car was waiting for Bajeux and Benoit! Bajeux did nearly all the talking; he said it was necessary for KONAKOM to distance itself from us. Victor, who said almost nothing, seemed nervous and upset. It was obvious that Bajeux — fronting for the State Department — was running the show.

Two days later (and just 48 hours before the end of the period for candidate registration), Aristide, the most popular grassroots leader in Haiti, announced his candidacy for the presidency with the backing of the FNCD.

"No one knows how Aristide conceives the presidency, and that is the danger of the affair," said Jean-Claude Bajeux, a left-leaning former Roman Catholic priest and longtime human rights leader who is not associated with any political campaign. "Now that Aristide is out front, he is obliged to negotiate with the bourgeoisie, but he reassures no one."

— *NEW YORK TIMES*, DECEMBER 13, 1990

Bajeux and Benoit were miffed. They would not support Aristide, and even tried to persuade KONAKOM's local candidates not to run on the same ticket with him. Although many of the local candidates ignored them, enough elections were forfeited so that the FNCD didn't have a majority in the National Assembly; President Aristide was thereby denied control over the legislature, seriously weakening his position — a situation that helped pave the way for the coup that drove him from office. During this time I made a strong effort to get in touch with Aristide to offer whatever support we could give, but was unable to reach him.

It was becoming disturbingly obvious that Bajeux was not what he had seemed: why would a Haitian leftist be worried about what was good for Washington?

We redoubled our efforts to reach Aristide. After his landslide victory in the election, I sent him a telegram of congratulations and, some time later, a letter telling him everything that had gone down with Bajeux — my intention was to warn Aristide, who for all his militance and courage was a small town priest with no experience of international politics. I never received a response to my letter.

But now, in the time since he was deposed by a rebellious army on Sept. 30, many who had supported the eight-month presidency of Father Aristide say the collapse of Haiti's brief experiment with democracy was hastened by an insular and menacing leader who saw his own raw popularity as a substitute for the give and take of politics…"For Lavalas, the Parliament became a negation of the power the people gave Aristide," said Jean-Claude Bajeux, a human rights advocate whose organization, Konakom, had supported the priest's candidacy. "They reasoned that Aristide should have had all the power because he was the people."

— *NEW YORK TIMES*, **OCTOBER 22, 1991**

When the coup came, on September 30, 1991, we were out in the streets with the Haitian people. It had become clear that, knowingly or not, the Haitian left (or pseudo-left) had helped to set Aristide up. Now, instead of closing ranks behind him, Bajeux and other so-called leftists took the opportunity to attack Aristide publicly by citing human rights violations that had taken place during the eight months of his presidency — and got themselves interviewed about it in the U.S. media! They were rationalizing the coup to the American people in the pages of the *New York Times,* thereby ensuring that he would not return easily — or at all. More than a year later, Aristide had yet to be restored to his rightful place as Haiti's president.

Following the coup, thousands of Haitians tried to flee the country, taking their lives in their hands. The U.S. Coast Guard began immediately intercepting those who fled, holding them at the U.S. military base at Guantanamo Bay in Cuba or forcibly returning them to Haiti, where many faced the wrath of the Macoutes. In November, I traveled twice to Miami for rallies at the invitation of Rolande Dorancy, the executive director of the Haitian Refugee Center there. Her own family had fled Baby Doc's regime a decade earlier, and she and her center have become known as "the voice of the Haitian refugee community." At the second rally, I addressed 8,000 people in the streets, taking the time to teach about our democracy movement, and how the kind of clout that, for example, the Zairian democracy movement has developed by virtue of our relationship to it can be wielded to return Aristide to the presidency. By the end of the rally, thousands of Haitians joined me for a chant of "Aristide in, Mobutu out!"

Send 'Em Back!: Washington says that U.S. doors are still open, but Haitian refugees are not its kind of huddled masses

— *TIME,* JUNE 8, 1992

In February, while I was campaigning in New Hampshire, Reverend Sharpton asked for our help in organizing a fact-finding trip to Haiti for Black ministers and others to investigate the dangers the Haitian refugees would face if they were forced to go back. He knew that we had international contacts and friends like Rolande Dorancy in Miami who could facilitate the trip. Fred immediately said yes.

I joined the contingent, which in addition to Reverend Sharpton included Alton Maddox, Reverend Darryl George from Mount Vernon, New York and Michael Hardy.

I was very sensitive to the fact that we needed to do whatever we did in Miami on whatever terms Rolande and the other leaders of the Haitian community thought were appropriate, because this was their struggle. And Miami was also their turf; we didn't in any way want to be disrespectful of them. I think Rev was disgruntled by this at first, but he was a big hit in Little Haiti. People understood the importance of his being there, and the media were all over the place. We were supposed to come back through there together on our way back, which didn't happen because Rev decided to stay on in Haiti an extra day. But I did stop in Miami on my way back to New Hampshire and spoke at a rally which was attended by about 3,000 people.

I talked about how the Haitian community could use my independent presidential campaign to force the issue of the refugees, and of Aristide's return, onto the political agenda. The crowd loved it. But the leadership was not receptive. For one thing, the refugee center was partly funded by the federal government — which meant that there were all sorts of restrictions and stipulations about participating in electoral politics.

There was a major Haitian rally in New York just before the primary in April. The Democratic Party flew in Maxine Waters, the California congresswoman, a protege of Jesse Jackson, to make a stump speech for Bill Clinton. My office was told that none of the candidates would be allowed to attack any of the others — which was basically to say that I couldn't speak the truth about Clinton. (This was right around the time when I ran him out of Harlem.)

I was so infuriated after listening to Maxine and the rest of the Clinton bandwagon! When I got up to speak I said that I wasn't supposed to attack any of the other candidates, so I wouldn't say anything about Jerry Brown, Bill Clinton or George Bush — because I thought they were all liars. The crowd roared. Then I told them why they had to go independent.

I challenge the Haitian American community not to be cheerleaders for the Democratic Party if they want to advance the struggle for Aristide's return and the fight for democracy in Haiti. There are a lot of forces conspiring against the Haitian people — including some of their supposed friends. But as far as I'm concerned, the final chapter on Haitian democracy has not yet been written.

The New Alliance Party has maintained sympathetic support for the Libyan regime of Col. Muamar Quaddafi. Dr. Lenora Fulani headed a New Alliance Party delegation at an "international Peace gathering" in Tripoli on April 14, 1987 to "commemorate...the genocidal U.S. bombing of the Gulf of Sidra and the Libyan coast."

> — *THE NEW ALLIANCE PARTY: A STUDY IN DECEPTION*,
> AN ADL RESEARCH REPORT, PUBLISHED BY THE
> ANTI-DEFAMATION LEAGUE OF B'NAI B'RITH, 1990

I went to Libya in April of 1987 with a contingent of Black nationalist and left organizations to attend an International Peace Gathering in commemoration of the American bombings of Tripoli and Benghazi a year earlier. We wanted to express our solidarity with the Libyan people and to share our outrage that under Ronald Reagan the U.S. government had murdered Muammar Qaddafi's 15-month-old baby in the attack on Benghazi. We were invited by Akbar Muhammad of the

Nation of Islam, on Qaddafi's behalf. We stayed in Libya for about four days.

The pretext for the bombing was that the Libyans had supposedly blown up a discotheque in Germany; it was later discovered that they hadn't. What was so infuriating was that there was no acknowledgement on the part of Washington that real human beings had been murdered. There was no acknowledgement that an atrocity had been committed. Most people in this country still don't know that the excuse the Reagan administration gave for blowing up the country was false, because no to-do was ever made about it.

I traveled with a small group of colleagues, among them Michael Hardy; Abukari, then a photographer for the *National Alliance* newspaper; Emilie Knoerzer, an assistant to Fred; and the Rainbow Lobby's Nancy Ross. The Libyans were extremely impressed that Nancy, a Jewish woman, was making a pro-Arab statement and in particular was supporting Qaddafi.

While we were there we met with many different groups, and talked to many people. Not surprisingly (because this is how the left, Black or white, typically conducts itself), no sooner had we arrived than many of the Black leftists began holding meetings at which the main order of business was to critique Qaddafi's *Green Book,* which contains his philosophy, including his views on politics. It's crazy — you don't go into somebody's country and tell them you don't like their philosophy. I went to a few of the meetings without getting into the fights.

One of the most exciting experiences I had was marching through the streets of Tripoli with the very militant young people of Libya. I loved it. Later, we took a trip into the mountains outside of Tripoli, where our hosts served us a traditional Arab meal of couscous. While we were there, I had a chance to speak with a group of Libyan women, who were very warm and very open about the progress women had made since the Libyan revolution.

You may never have heard of Lenora B. Fulani, the presidential candidate of the New Alliance Party, but your tax dollars are paying for her anti-Jewish and pro-Libyan campaign. So far Ms. Fulani's tiny party has collected checks totaling $763,928 in federal matching funds. The story of the New Alliance Party is a cautionary tale for those who think public financing of elections would invigorate U.S. politics. More likely, it would only make it fringier.

— *WALL STREET JOURNAL*, FEBRUARY 5, 1992

I've been attacked ever since for going — whenever the people who hate NAP want to stir the pot. During the New Hampshire primary the *Wall Street Journal* quoted heavily from the Anti-Defamation League's charges about my "Libya connection" in its editorial attacking me and public campaign financing. We took a very strong stand against the invasion and the bombing, which the people of this country had not supported. In fact, the American people didn't even know it was happening. The U.S. military just made a surprise move. It was yet another example of the ongoing assault on people of color internationally when they differ with the U.S. government, or they identify the wrongs of imperialism. I was trying to teach our people that Qaddafi was another of Uncle Sam's bogeymen — someone the powers-that-be had decided was a "bad guy" so they could do anything they wanted to do to him. What would it mean for the U.S. to express its differences with the government of a sovereign nation such as France by flying into Paris and blowing up the French president's residence? I have worked to educate people about how the policies of our government do not endear us to the rest of humanity — in fact there had been marches all over the world, in England, Germany and other places, to protest the bombing.

The trip was a stretch for me, politically; traveling to Libya is not your run-of-the-mill trip. It expanded my horizons, putting NAP right in the middle of a fight on the side of a controversial Third World leader who had the guts to stand up to the U.S., even though his country was small, and fight for the empowerment of people of color. We continue to have a relationship with Libya and have made it clear to Libyans in the U.S. that we will be very outspoken in our defense of their country. I recently went to a reception at the Libyan Mission for their new representative to the UN, Dr. Ali Ahmed Elhouderi. (I had a close working relationship with Dr. Ali Treiki, the former UN representative, who later became the Libyan ambassador to the United Arab League in Cairo.)

A number of left organizations in the United States have related to the Libyans as a bank. But we haven't sought them out to get money from them. I've invited them into the African American community here because I wanted to give them the opportunity to make a connection with people of color in this country, as a way to mobilize support for their struggle by letting our communities get to know them better. They've not been particularly open to that. They've been cordial — they'll send a person here, a person there, to a demonstration or a meeting — but not in the full spirit of recognizing that they can use the independent political movement in this country to strengthen their fight.

At the reception for the new ambassador, I introduced myself to him, and he said, "Oh, Dr. Fulani, you don't have to introduce yourself to me. I know all about you. You're a famous lady." But when I suggested that we have a meeting, he just smiled at me.

Since 1959 — when I began graduate school and the people of Cuba began socialism — I have devoted almost all of my intellectual energies, as well as my practical energies, to the study of two things: psychology and revolution.

—FRED NEWMAN, *THE MYTH OF PSYCHOLOGY*, 1991

In June of 1987 — the day after I announced that I was running for president — I went to Cuba with several colleagues including Fred; Gail Elberg, NAP's dynamic New York coordinator; Mary Rivera and Jeff Aron, who were then with the Rainbow Lobby; and Dr. Lois Holzman, the friend and colleague who first introduced me to Fred; we had been invited to participate in the biannual gathering of the Interamerican Congress of Psychology, which was held in the Karl Marx Theatre in Havana. Fred gave a talk on "the psychopathology of the U.S. left," and I spoke about the intimate relationship of politics and psychology.

I loved being in Cuba — I felt frustrated by not being able to speak Spanish, but it was still wonderful and inspiring. It was also sad: the Cuban people made a revolution, but the U.S. government is determined that they not reap anything from it.

We had several meetings with representatives of the Central Committee of the Cuban Communist Party while we were in Havana, at which we told them how we viewed the political movement coming into existence that would one day be a major third party in the United States.

Fred spoke a lot with us about the care and work that have

to go into being able to communicate with folks. When I first got to Cuba I was talking about NAP as being "women of color-led." It was so idiosyncratic — people didn't know what I was talking about!

On this trip Fred taught us about being internationalists. We had a very intimate discussion one night when he told us that as an internationalist he would go anyplace in the world where he thought he could be most useful to the international working class, wherever his presence would have the most impact — that he wasn't committed to being a leftist in the United States. That was sobering.

The trip ended up being an intensive, 10-day, 24-hour-a-day political lesson for those of us who went. I was still new, in many ways, to international politics; I was both intimidated by it and arrogant toward it. And I was very green in terms of knowing the left, and more particularly the international left. The dialogues we had with Cuban political leaders made it clear that their only knowledge of the American scene was derived from the very distorted information given to them by the Communist Party U.S.A., which had led them to believe that the Democratic Party is a progressive, working-class party!

Of course, it is precisely [his] list of accomplishments as a U.S. ally in the region that has earned Mobutu the unending ire of Capitol Hill, or, more precisely, the ire of those on the Hill who matter most when it comes to U.S. policy on Africa...They in turn are affected mightily by the Rainbow Lobby, a New York based anti-Mobutu outfit. This crowd's basic beef is simple enough: they don't like U.S. policy on Africa, of which Zaire is a lynchpin. And since they cannot win a fair and square policy victory — for example, ending U.S. aid to Savimbi's UNITA

— they beat up on Mobutu and run Africa policy on the sly through a cornucopia of legislative restrictions.

— *AMERICAN SPECTATOR*, FEBRUARY 1990

Bending to public outrage, Mr. Mobutu's representatives have been meeting with opposition leaders since July 1991 in a national political conference intended to draft a new constitution and set a schedule for multiparty elections. This month the delegates began drafting a new constitution enshrining a multiparty system and elected Etienne Tschisekedi [sic], Mr. Mobutu's most prominent opponent, as prime minister of a transitional government.

— *NEW YORK TIMES*, AUGUST 30, 1992

Over the last several years NAP and I have worked with the Rainbow Lobby, a grassroots citizens' lobby for democracy, to mobilize support among the American people and in Congress for the struggle of the Zairian people against the dictatorship of Mobutu Sese Seko. A former officer in the Belgian colonial army, Mobutu came to power in 1965, four years after he conspired with the CIA to assassinate Patrice Lumumba, the only popularly elected prime minister of the Congo (as Zaire was then called). During 27 years as his country's self-appointed president-for-life, Mobutu has amassed a personal fortune of $5 billion — while the people of Zaire, one of the richest countries on earth in natural resources, have become the poorest of the world's poor people (one out of every two children under the age of five dies of starvation or preventable diseases).

Together, NAP and the Rainbow Lobby have taken the struggle of the Zairian people from being completely unknown to the American people to the point where even the *New York Times* sees "fit to print" news about it.

What we've been able to do with Zaire is an example of how you can be small and poor (by Washington standards) and still make a difference, a dent. The key to our success is our independence. Neither the Lobby nor NAP is beholden to those who have an interest in keeping Mobutu in power. For a generation the Democratic Party effectively collaborated with the Republican Party to protect Mobutu as America's chief ally in Africa against the "communist threat"; more recently, with the coming of Bush's "new world order," Washington has promoted Mobutu as a friend of democracy, an "elder statesman" who all but singlehandedly brought an end to the 14-year-old civil war in Angola. In fact Mobutu had been instrumental in fomenting tensions in Angola on behalf of the U.S. State Department and the South African regime. We've been able to wage this fight in support of our Zairian sisters and brothers consistently and ruthlessly. We've given the people of Zaire material, moral and political support; they know that they aren't alone. With that support the Zairians have gone a very long way. That's not to say that they are free yet. But their struggle is much more familiar to people in this country, which makes it a lot harder for Washington to support Zaire's dictator. We have relentlessly forced the issue into the open in the face of much Democratic Party liberal stonewalling, outright opposition and mudslinging.

In May of 1989 NAP and the Rainbow Lobby succeeded in disrupting a public relations stunt designed to bring Mobutu into the African American community, concealed in the "Trojan horse" of the Gevakin Choir. The choir, whose name derives from the first letters of Gospel Evangelical of Kinshasa, the capital city of Zaire, was on a three-month, 50-city tour of Black

Baptist churches in the Northeast and Midwest. The tour was sponsored by the American Baptist Foreign Missionary Society, which has operated a large number of missions in Zaire for more than a century. As soon as we got wind of the tour, I wrote a letter to Black ministers around New York City and New York state in which I said, "The tour is being used as part of a propaganda campaign by the regime of Mobutu Sese Seko designed to convince the American people that this brutal dictator and friend of apartheid is a humane and progressive leader who deserves our support and respect. Nothing could be further from the truth." I specifically mentioned that the choir had already appeared at the 19th Street Baptist Church in Washington, whose pastor had just been appointed ambassador to Lesotho by President Bush, and that Representative Mervyn Dymally — the Black "liberal" congressman from California who acted as Mobutu's mouthpiece on Capitol Hill — was in the pulpit that Sunday morning to put in a good word for Mobutu with the congregation.

I warned them that if they were going to have people from Zaire singing spirituals they should also take responsibility for informing their congregations about conditions in Zaire under Mobutu and about the democratic opposition to his dictatorship.

Needless to say, some of these ministers weren't happy with me for making a commotion about this: some men of the cloth think they don't have to be accountable for their actions. Ivan George, the board president of the International Ministries of American Baptists, called me on the phone and tried to bully me into backing off. He said I had no right to criticize Mobutu since I had never been to Zaire. Well, I was never in Nazi Germany either, but I have an obligation to make moral and political judgments about the evils committed by and under

Hitler. And I never lived under slavery but that does not stop me from expressing my moral indignation about it.

One of the ministers I lobbied most persistently was the Reverend Calvin Butts, the pastor of the Abyssinian Baptist Church in Harlem. It was in Abyssinian that Adam Clayton Powell, who would become the first Black congressman since Reconstruction, instilled pride and a spirit of resistance in a generation of Black people. Reverend Butts, who cultivates his reputation as a "militant," never responded to my letter. He welcomed the Gevakin Choir to Abyssinian; the congregation was not told beforehand that the choir would be there. Reverend Butts and some of his colleagues took the attitude that the choir had nothing to do with Mobutu. Of course, that was nonsense; nobody could even get out of Zaire unless Mobutu gave the okay.

Having been brought up in the Baptist Church, I know that Christians have an obligation to speak out about human suffering. I believe very strongly that ministers are just as responsible for what they do as anybody else.

I said this in a presentation I made at the Manhattan Baptist Ministers Day Conference, urging them to take a stand against Mobutu's "holy" ambassadors in the Gevakin Choir. Before I was allowed to speak to the whole group, a committee of ministers interviewed me. "Dr. Fulani, the ministers want to know if you believe in God," they said. When they finally let me address the whole body, I said it wasn't my beliefs that should be questioned but the beliefs of the men of God who were allowing an unholy statement to be made in their churches, in their names, when the Zairian people were dying. "You can't hide behind red-baiting me to cover over what these men are doing," I told them. "Why aren't you asking Calvin Butts, the minister of one of New York City's largest churches, who and what he believes in? Whatever his beliefs are, they certainly aren't helping the Zairian people."

I am not — in any sense — "one of the boys." With some honorable exceptions, the official Black leadership — particularly Democratic Party elected officials and clergymen — relate to me as an intruder on their turf; they think I'm "uppity." Frankly, I'm not concerned with their opinion of me. I have no intention of ever shutting up, or letting up. My job is to teach people the truth about what's going on in our country and the world, so that we can change it.

Atlantic City mayor James L. Usry...said he didn't "give a damn" about the Rainbow Lobby, and added that the group should spend its time working against the government of South Africa. In fact, it is doing just that...Perhaps Usry isn't aware that Zaire actually has close contacts with South Africa...We'd like to think that Usry and the National Conference of Black Mayors would want nothing to do with a despotic regime; the fact that its leaders are black doesn't excuse the despotism. It's blacks in Zaire who are victims of that despotism.

— *ATLANTIC CITY PRESS*, JUNE 12, 1989

On June 19, 1989 members of the Atlanta-based National Conference of Black Mayors, along with other Black elected officials and businesspeople, were scheduled to go on a two- week visit to Zaire. I sent a letter to the mayors urging them to cancel the all-expenses-paid-by-Mobutu trip: "In no way can we, as African American leaders, particularly Black elected officials, give any semblance of support to Mobutu Sese Seko," I wrote. The mayors were also contacted — and urged to cancel their trip — by the American Friends Service Committee, the

Southern Africa Resource Center, and the Rainbow Lobby.

We caught a lot of flak for "interfering" with the mayors' excursion. In doing so we exposed the lack of sophistication within the Black community and how Mobutu — with Representative Dymally's help — manipulated the naiveté of local Black elected officials, as well as their racism toward their African sisters and brothers, for his own purposes. (An example of such racism was the announcement by the mayor of East St. Louis that he was taking his own blood supply to Zaire so he wouldn't run any risk of having to receive a transfusion of "monkey blood.")

We created such a ruckus in the media over the trip that at the last minute James Usry, the mayor of Atlantic City and at the time the chairman of the Black mayors organization, announced that he wasn't going (he cited "medical problems" and a prior commitment to serve as a judge in the Miss Tennessee beauty contest to explain his change of plans) and the junketeers dwindled down from the original 19 to a handful. We had succeeded in serving notice to Mobutu and his American patrons that there was a coordinated movement in this country which would stymie every effort to peddle him in the African American community.

"Keep Out Of Harlem," New Alliance Party's Dr. Lenora Fulani warned Zaire's President Mobutu Sese Seko Wednesday morning, as she led some 200 marchers from 125th St. and Seventh Avenue to join a coalition-sponsored demonstration at the U.N., timed for Mobutu's address to the General Assembly.

— NEW YORK *AMSTERDAM NEWS*, OCTOBER 14, 1989

In October of 1989 I led a march from Harlem to the United Nations to protest Mobutu's appearance at the General

Assembly. Our action was a re-creation of the famous march from Harlem 28 years earlier, when hundreds of people went to the UN to protest the CIA-orchestrated assassination of Lumumba. Now the people of Harlem were once again standing up to defend their Congolese sisters and brothers.

On our way, we marched past Zaire's mission to the UN. We stopped, and chanted, "Mobutu is a murderer!" Mobutu's thugs came downstairs and began chanting back at us. It was a very intense confrontation. The police showed up and made us move on. We continued to the UN and held a rally in the area reserved for demonstrations.

Then six of us — including Hazel Daren, who was then the director of the U.S.-Congo Friendship Committee, Rafael Mendez, my special assistant, and Sister Leontine O'Gorman, a human rights activist — walked over to the UN, went inside and up to the visitors' gallery where the General Assembly was in session. I waited until Mobutu started speaking. Then I stood up and yelled out, "Mobutu is a murderer! Long live the spirit of Patrice Lumumba and the Congolese people!" The rest of our contingent stood up and chanted with me. Mobutu stopped speaking. By some lucky fluke, this whole episode was shown on Zairian television — their cameraman shot it and someone, by mistake, let it go on the air in Zaire. It was a very big deal for the Zairian people. At a time when no one was speaking out against Mobutu — even the most progressive governments in Africa couldn't, because it was against the policy of the Organization of African Unity — they saw Black, Latino and white Americans, in the United Nations, shut the tyrant up! (I received many letters from Zaire telling me how moralized people were by what we had done.)

After a minute or so, security guards grabbed us and took

us down to the basement. The head of security wanted to put us into a holding area enclosed by bars. Hazel started screaming that we wouldn't go, and there was a huge commotion. They finally decided not to put us behind bars, and after about an hour we were allowed to leave.

I was very proud of the homeless people from Harlem who marched with us, for giving something to the Congolese people's struggle. Even without housing, without any of the things that they needed in their own lives, they were able to see the significance of this fight and join in.

Mr. DYMALLY. Mr. Speaker, as part of my effort to expose a campaign of harassment against me by the U.S.-Congo Friendship Committee, Hazel Daren, coordinator; the New Alliance Party and the Rainbow Lobby, I bring to the attention of Members some background information about the organizations and individuals involved in this campaign of harassment.

— REP. MERVYN M. DYMALLY,
CONGRESSIONAL RECORD, JULY 20, 1990

We're independents. Our hands aren't tied. If we think a move is important, we make it; we're not compromised. An example of this is the intense fight we had with Mervyn Dymally. He tried to use Black nationalism to cover over his complicity in the slaughter of Zairian people. For years Dymally acted as a spokesman for Mobutu on Capitol Hill. The African American community — which has been misled by the Black left and the Black nationalists — is very susceptible to the notion that Mobutu, who dresses in traditional African garb and renamed everything (including Zaire's currency, the "zaire") with "authentic" tribal names, couldn't possibly be a torturer and a murderer of African people. But Mobutu is exactly that.

Dymally — who at one time was the chairman of the Congressional Black Caucus — used his position as a U.S. congressman to function as a middleman for the international diamond industry, which couldn't be any whiter. Under the pretext of defending African Americans' right to have the same relationship to Africa that Jews have to Israel, Dymally increased his personal influence by serving as a go-between for assorted high rollers and wheeler-dealers in this country and the Mobutu-run "kleptocracy." To protect himself and his business friends, Dymally had to keep the American people, particularly the Black community, ignorant of what was happening in Zaire. So he defended Mobutu. He covered for him; he lied for him.

The Rainbow Lobby and the New Alliance Party took on the job of exposing Dymally. We were severely criticized for that, by Dymally himself and by other Black Democrats and liberals who lacked the courage to speak out against Dymally or defend us against his attacks. In 1987 Ron Dellums, the California congressman, introduced H.R. 3355, a bill drafted by the Rainbow Lobby which called for cutting off aid to Mobutu unless there was a drastic improvement in the human rights situation in Zaire. (Its provisions were later incorporated into the foreign aid appropriations bill that was passed in the fall of 1990.) But even he wouldn't go all the way when it came to violating the rules of "professional courtesy" toward another Black Democrat; like his colleagues, Dellums refused to take a stand in our fight with Dymally.

Dellums, Randall Robinson, who heads TransAfrica, and the leaders of the South Africa solidarity organizations keep their distance from us under the guise of not wanting to endanger the struggle in South Africa. This is confusing to people, because they expect Robinson and Dellums and the others to take a stand when the lives of African people are in jeopardy. Dellums, Robinson and Co. use the excuse that they don't like the people who are leading the fight: NAP and the Rainbow Lobby. But we're leading the fight *because* they wouldn't take it on — that's why the Zairians came to us in the first place. And that's why Etienne Tshisekedi, who later became the prime minister of Zaire, stepped into the fray and defended us.

Wherever I went throughout the country during my 1988 campaign (as well as before and afterward) I made a point of teaching people that Dymally was a traitor to Black people everywhere. There is no justification, in my opinion, for protecting such Black "leaders." Meanwhile, Dymally was crying "Racism!" and insisting that this was yet another case of a Black elected official — himself — being targeted for attack by "racists." But in fact we weren't "attacking" Mervyn Dymally — we were exposing the fact that this particular Black elected official and some of his friends were in bed with an African dictator who would stop at nothing to hold on to his ill-gotten wealth and power. We let Dymally know that he couldn't scare us off: we would scream even louder about his complicity in the murder of the Congolese people, and he would have to live with that because their blood is on his hands.

In the spring of 1990 NAP backed Lawrence Grigsby, an African American attorney, in his Democratic Party primary challenge to Dymally in California's 31st Congressional District. It was really exciting to campaign for Grigsby against Dymally in Compton, one of the poorest Black districts in the country. We got on the back of a flatbed truck and rode through the streets, teaching people about the "Compton-Congo connection." This was not New York; people weren't used to the kind of campaigning NAP does in the street:

"Mervyn Dymally is participating in the slaughter of the Congolese people! You have a responsibility to make this statement for the Zairian people, because they aren't in a position to say anything themselves. You can make that statement by voting for Lawrence Grigsby on primary day!"

People heard that; they were intrigued; they had never seen anything like this. Many of them didn't even know who their congressman was, and the ones who knew Dymally didn't particularly like him. They understood why it was important to speak out on behalf of African people. Lawrence ended up with over 15% of the vote in the primary.

I briefed Minister Farrakhan on the situation in Zaire, and Dymally's role in it. I wanted him to know what the real deal was, given all the lies that Dymally was circulating. At one point the Minister spoke to me about arranging a meeting between Dymally and me. He said Dymally had suggested it. But that meeting never came off; Dymally didn't pursue it.

During our long struggle, we have had an opportunity to appreciate the support of our friends abroad...We recognize the unrelenting effort by the Rainbow Lobby and its executive director, Ms. Nancy Ross, as well as by her colleagues in support of our cause...Meanwhile, Mr. Mobutu's friends and supporters in the United States, including Representative Dymally...have continued to carry out a campaign of misinformation designed to mislead the American people about Mr. Mobutu's oppressive and corrupt regime and to gather support for increased U.S. financial aid to Mr. Mobutu.

— FROM A LETTER WRITTEN BY ETIENNE TSHISEKEDI
AND HAND-DELIVERED TO EVERY MEMBER OF CONGRESS,
AUGUST 10, 1990

Unlike the struggle against apartheid in South Africa, Zaire has never been a "legitimate" fight. Try telling the people of Zaire that the U.S. left has turned its back on them because their struggle is not officially sanctioned in progressive circles, or because the moribund Communist Party U.S.A. and its hangers-on don't like NAP! In order to wage this fight on behalf of the Congolese people, we had to take on not only a Black head of state (Mobutu) and his fascist regime — we had to take on a powerful Black congressman (Dymally) who was covering for the dictator, and the Black elected officials who wouldn't buck him. We raised some very serious issues for a lot of people.

We were Jew-baited; we were red-baited; we were cult-baited. Politicians related to the Rainbow Lobby as if it had the plague. But Nancy Ross and Deborah Green refused to back off on the principle that if you're fighting fascism, then you should fight those people who are participating in it — even if they cloak themselves in liberalism or nationalism.

Zaire's democratic opposition to Mobutu doesn't have an orthodox left — it has been destroyed. That's not to say that the Zairians don't need a left, but the democratic opposition in Zaire isn't controlled and constrained by the "manual" co-authored by the Communist Party and the orthodox left and the Democratic Party on how to fight.

In November of 1990 I hosted a reception for the Zairian democrats who were in Washington for a conference on "Prospects for Democracy in Zaire." The conference was co-sponsored by the Rainbow Lobby, the Center for Research on Zaire, the Department of African Studies at Howard University and the International Center for Development Policy. It was an extremely moving occasion; some people there were seeing each other again after many years of not knowing whether their comrades had died in Mobutu's prisons. I said I was a "student" of the Congolese struggle, and expressed my gratitude for being allowed to contribute to it. Tshisekedi, who gave one of the two keynote addresses at the conference, smilingly took it upon himself to speak for all his countrymen present. He graciously refused my thanks. "On the contrary," he said, "it is we who should be thanking you, and the Rainbow Lobby, for all you have done."

When the New Alliance Party held its nominating convention in August of 1992, Tshisekedi — who two weeks earlier had been elected prime minister by the Sovereign National Conference — sent the following message of solidarity to us: "Please accept my warmest greetings and congratulations to you and all of the delegates...You have my best wishes as you examine how to expand democracy in the United States and to support democratic and progressive forces all over the world. We appreciate the outstanding work that you, your party and the Rainbow Lobby have done on behalf of our struggle for democracy in Zaire. We will continue to work with you to develop stronger and mutually beneficial relations between the peoples of our respective countries."

In accepting NAP's presidential nomination, I began by paying tribute to the accomplishments of our Congolese sisters and brothers. Their courage has been an enormous source of inspiration to me personally. When you are building an independent political movement in this country, and every day you are forced to face, not the physical torture that the Congolese people have had to face but political abuse — "Oh, Dr. Fulani. She's nothing but a kook." "Oh, the New Alliance Party. That's nothing but a cult." "Oh, Fred Newman. He's nothing but a brainwasher" — when you have to face this kind of attack, when the FBI is "investigating" you and circulating false reports that you are "armed and dangerous," you sometimes feel frightened for yourself and for your kids.

When I feel that way, I think of the Congolese women who've had to raise their children and care for their families and work a job (when they could find one) in the midst of great fear and tremendous social upheaval. I think of how the Congolese people stood firm with their simple message: YOU WILL NOT DISRUPT THIS DEMOCRATIC PROCESS. I am made strong by that. It enables me to say to the Democrats and Republicans, to the FBI, to the white leftists and the Black leftists and everyone else who wants to tarnish or destroy what we are building: YOU WILL NOT DISRUPT THIS DEMOCRATIC PROCESS.

Tshisekedi isn't a creature of the Democratic Party. The Rainbow Lobby brought him to the United States and lobbied on his behalf in Congress, and NAP took his cause to the streets of Black America, as part of our efforts to build a relationship between the masses of the Congolese people and the people of this country. When Tshisekedi returns to the United States to negotiate with Washington as the leader of his country, he will be able to continue to use his relationship with us to maintain some independence at the bargaining table (that's why the U.S. State Department isn't in love with him).

It is through NAP's involvement in the struggle to overthrow the Mobutu dictatorship that I have gotten to know Dr. Georges Nzongola-Ntalaja, a Zairian intellectual and activist who lived in exile here for many years. In the spring of 1992, Georges returned home to Zaire as a delegate to the Sovereign National Conference.

At my invitation he had come to Harlem several times in the last few years to give us a blow-by-blow description — and more recently, after his first return home, an eyewitness account — of the fight to get Mobutu out. Unlike many intellectuals and activists Georges is both a genuine democrat and a genuine internationalist.

In April of 1991 I organized a march and rally in Harlem to

demonstrate the support of the African American community for our Congolese sisters and brothers, who were risking their lives by organizing strikes and protests against the dictatorship. Mobutu had sent troops against unarmed demonstrators, and it was urgent that the Zairian people be sent a message of solidarity from the American people. Georges was the featured speaker at the rally. Then, in September of 1991, Georges and I spoke at another rally, this time at the UN, which the Rainbow Lobby and NAP held to call attention to the situation in Zaire. Mobutu had, for the time being, forcibly closed down the National Conference, and the leaders of the "Sacred Union of the Opposition," a coalition of democratic forces in Zaire, were appealing to the international community for support in preventing a bloodbath which they feared was imminent.

In the spring of 1992 — about a month before he went back to Zaire — Georges came to New York to participate in "Democracy Dialogue '92." Delegations from El Salvador, Mexico, Puerto Rico, Colombia, Argentina, the Philippines, Senegal, the Ivory Coast and Mali as well as Zaire took part in this three-day conference, which I hosted; its purpose was to get input from pro-democracy forces on the foreign policy platform of my presidential campaign. We had the opportunity to meet again when I was in Washington at the end of August of 1992 to attend the founding convention of the 21st Century Party and Georges was back in town to wind up his affairs.

Georges is one of the most courageous and principled people I know. I assured him that NAP will continue to bring the struggle of the Congolese people to the forefront. That's what we independents do. We barge into places, uninvited and unwanted, stand up, and insist at the top of our lungs that poor people — the ones the powers-that-be think are too illegitimate to fight for — are going to be heard...whether they're in

Harlem or Kinshasa. We're going to keep on fighting like hell for our Zairian sisters and brothers in the way that makes the loudest noise and the biggest bang — whether the folks in high places and their minions like it or not.

II

AIN'T I A WOMAN!

Chester, a small industrial town on the Delaware River, is really an old city which for years had its own Republican machine; most of its residents are black now.

— *THE ALMANAC OF AMERICAN POLITICS 1988*

My mother, who's now in her seventies, was 35 when I was born in 1950. She still lives in Chester, Pennsylvania with my sister Shirley. I go to Chester to visit them two or three times a year. When I first became politically active, they didn't quite know what to make of me. But they've come to terms with my lifestyle. It isn't what they'd call "normal." Maybe they have some judgments and opinions about my untraditional life, but they give me space. They weren't sure about what I was doing when I first joined NAP, or when I left my husband Richard. I had come to New York City (a longer way from Chester than just the miles indicate!) and done well there. I made a life for myself and my kids. And I'm something of a celebrity. My cousin Yvonne told a reporter who was interviewing her about me, "She was always somebody."

I learned a lot from the women in my family about being a working-class woman, being a mover, being able to take care of myself and my children. Shirley, my sister, taught me that I *had* to fight. My cousin Vonnie taught me that college could be more than a far-off dream. And my mother, who only completed the sixth grade, was a model for me of a Black woman who takes extraordinary risks. I love them all dearly. And these lessons are still very much alive in me.

I come from a family of poor, working-class Black women who managed to survive. My sisters and cousins had babies early and were responsible for raising them. Even when I was little, I knew it was my mother who kept us alive.

Still, the work I did in therapy on sexism was harder for me than anything else. It felt more like giving something up — giving up using sex and sexual attractiveness to negotiate with men (women always end up on the losing side). I had a tough, feminist veneer which I thought protected me, but men used to slay me left and right. I would believe things they said that I would never have believed in other situations, when my brain worked properly.

We did a lot of work on my "toughness," which wasn't toughness, but vulnerability to men. I couldn't bear to hear that. I still don't like to hear it. But this is always an issue, because there's an ongoing conflict between the myth we've all been taught — you have to be a certain kind of woman for men to give you anything — and the reality of what women do and don't get from men.

I was the smartest girl in the sixth grade at my mostly Black school, and James Batton was the smartest boy. At the end of the year when they gave out awards James, who was Black, got the top boys' award and a white girl named Janet Lloyd got the top girls' award. Janet was also poor (she wouldn't have been in that school otherwise), but she was white. I was shocked by the lesson: if you're poor and Black, things can get taken away from you even if you deserve them. Although I knew the award should have gone to me, I didn't say anything about it to anyone. I was so humiliated and angry that I was upset about it for years. There was no one I could talk to about it — not even my mother. I was afraid I'd be called a sore loser.

The first 18 years of my life I was deeply immersed in the church. My rites of passage were all connected to the church: becoming an usher, giving the welcome address, playing the piano — I earned money playing for weddings and church feasts. It was during this time in church that I was trained to be a leader. I was outspoken, bright, opinionated. Soon, I ran everything. When I was 18, I made a conscious decision to leave the church — I decided to take what I had learned there into the community and give it to my people.

Growing up, working-class girls get very mixed messages. On the one hand we see that our grandmothers, mothers and aunts are smart, tough, and competent — often smarter, stronger, more able and more *there* than their men — and on the other hand we see that it is the men who have power. Women aren't allowed to speak our minds, let alone organize our lives and our environment on our terms; we are frequently treated (by women and men) as stupid; we are ignored, laughed at, and sometimes harmed if we step out of our "place."

Like many working-class Black women, I didn't grow up under the illusion that having a man would solve all my problems. From what I had seen of my mother's life and the lives of my sisters and my cousins, I concluded that you could love men, but you couldn't afford to rely on them — emotionally or economically. It was always the women in my life who kept everything together — even under incredibly difficult circumstances.

I am a woman who wants to exercise power and to teach other people (women and men) to exercise power (if I didn't, I wouldn't be doing what I do). In my experience, women often aren't very good at exercising power. That's not surprising. Since every institution in our society actively discourages us from being powerful, we don't get much practice. Even when we do want power, what dominates our actions is a male model of power — one which is abusive and inhumane. For women to be powerful on our own terms, we must create environments in which we're *supported* to exercise power — otherwise, we're made fools of...and worse.

I don't always agree with my feminist sisters, nor do they with me. Some feminist leaders have been outraged that my political mentor is a man, Fred Newman. (It's rather ironic, since for many years the women's movement has been locked into an abusive marriage with the male-led Democratic Party, which, in classic male tradition, takes women for granted while giving us virtually nothing in return.) Far from feeling defensive, I'm extremely proud that this particular man — a deeply committed working-class Jewish revolutionary — is behind me and every other powerful woman leader of NAP.

It's taken enormous work to create a political community in which women are challenged to develop as *leaders*. It's a community where women have power — so much power that when one of us decides to do "consciousness-raising" it's a step backward! (It's just not productive to challenge every single instance of sexism; if we did, we'd have to close up shop because there wouldn't be time to do anything else!) We are going all the way. The men who want to come with us are welcome — we both need and want them — but we're not waiting for their approval or their permission. Our people don't have time for us to wait.

Within the New Alliance Party we've had our own fights over the leadership of women. A major battle took place in 1985, when — under Fred's direction — I led the floor fight at NAP's national convention in Chicago that culminated in the takeover of our party by the women of color who had been working night and day for the previous six years to build it.

As in any war, this battle had many "proximate causes." One was Dennis Serrette, who left NAP in early 1985 shortly after he ran as our candidate for president of the United States.

Serrette adds that NAP is running Fulani this year...to give the illusion of Black leadership while Newman remains in actual control.

— KEN LAWRENCE, *GUARDIAN*, OCTOBER 19, 1988

For Serrette and me, it had been "love" at first sight. He always used to praise me for being a political woman who was also attractive, *and* who could understand him in ways other Black women hadn't been able to (which is how he explained his being in a million and one relationships with white women).

I was thrilled with Serrette at first: he was good-looking, smart, a leftist, and crazy about me. And Black. Unfortunately, all of these things helped to keep me from knowing who he really was.

What also helped was that I did with him what I had learned to do with men who wanted to make me into something I didn't want to be. I had learned that if you want to keep men in your life, you can't object to everything they say — but you also don't have to do what they want. They interpret silence as acquiescence. So I ignored Serrette when he said outrageous things. The problem with turning people off like that, saying "uh-huh" and going your own way, is that you don't learn who they are. You end up being in a relationship with someone you don't know and who doesn't know you.

Serrette did all the commonplace nasty things to me that

men do to women. He would call me up and tell me he'd be there on Tuesday, then not show up for three weeks. I was humiliated, but I wanted the relationship — so I put up with it, in silence. Then I started talking about it in therapy.

One of the things we worked on in my therapy group was my not waiting for him. I was relieved, because I could never have stopped this by myself. I started to be more and more public with the relationship, so all kinds of "secrets" got out. Fred was very critical of me for being furious with Serrette all the time. Women often end up having fights about petty, trivial things — which is just as degrading as being a doormat. Fred was also critical because it wasn't supportive of Serrette's political leadership — I would want to choke Fred at those times. He never patronized me — he just said what he thought about what was politically problematic or awkward.

Serrette hated it that I talked about our relationship in my therapy group. But I didn't know how much he hated it. He ended our relationship around Thanksgiving of 1983. We were sitting in a restaurant, and he made it short and sweet: "You're too political. I don't want somebody like you." I was crushed.

I called Fred that night and he asked, "Hasn't this been happening all along?"

I was shocked. "It has?" And of course it had been happening — I just hadn't recognized it. Serrette was competing for me politically — with Fred. I liked having sex with Serrette, and I had even allowed him to get to know my kids. But I'd never thought of leaving politics to be with him. I believed I could persuade Serrette to be open and decent. It took me more than three years to realize I couldn't do it.

I never want to go through an experience like that again. But what emerged from it was my development as an African American leader of our political movement — and NAP's development as a women of color-led organization, which many people still have not come to terms with, and some people just don't like.

"I left the party because it continued to claim it was Black led — I knew better," Serrette said. "I mean no harm to these powerful Black women, Emily Carter, Lenora Fulani and Barbara Taylor, when I say that. I knew from being there that they were not leading Fred Newman — he was leading them — that's why I left."

— DENNIS SERRETTE, *JACKSON* [MS] *ADVOCATE*, MAY 23, 1985

The moment he left NAP, Serrette embarked on a new career as a "source" for the professional NAP-bashers. Serrette now says he left when he discovered (after being in NAP for three years!) that NAP wasn't "really" Black-led. In fact, NAP was led by women of color who wouldn't do his bidding. He was never supportive of NAP's women of color leadership; our women of color caucus had frequent fights with him, in the course of which he would criticize and ridicule Emily Carter, Lorraine Stevens and me for being stupid and unsophisticated — mostly because we followed Fred. In my experience, Serrette didn't have any use for women unless he could get us into bed.

I could write 17 chapters on sex, politics and Dennis Serrette. He was very manipulative — maybe no more so than other men, but we were sexually involved at a point in my life when I faced a test: sex or politics. Or rather, what kind of sex? And what kind of politics?

Serrette and I had many fights about the kind of woman I ought to be. He expected me to be *his* woman first, and a political leader second. That was his condition for having a relationship with me; it was sexual blackmail. I learned a lot from that experience. At other times in my life, I could always cop out and go with "my man." Now I was a political leader, which changed everything.

I was involved with Serrette for three years. Our relationship was a protracted struggle. In the end, I'm sure he believed that I chose Fred over him. And he was right — I did.

When Serrette was first quoted in the *Jackson Advocate* (a Black-owned newspaper in Mississippi), attacking Fred and me, I felt violated. I was stunned that this man, whom I had allowed into my life and into the lives of my children, had tried to harm me. It taught me about sexual politics on the left, in general, and about his cowardice in particular.

One sexual dynamic on the left sets white women up as sexual prizes. Often they are prizes for Black men, who use the opportunity afforded by a socially liberal environment to have sex with them. Some progressive white women even take the position that if you sleep with Black men you're not racist. Many Black women I've spoken with feel victimized by this set-up. Fred taught me how to reorganize it rather than to be humiliated by it.

Right after the 1984 election NAP's Black leaders had a meeting with Fred (Serrette didn't bother to attend) during which we put all kinds of issues out on the table — including the manipulation of women that had gone down during the campaign. Among the things we talked about was Black men and white women in sexual relationships, and how they are often used to attack Black women.

We worked on why we as Black women, instead of providing leadership in such situations, acted as if they were the end of the world. In this context, we talked about Serrette (for some time he had been seeing Kathy Hollenberg, a Jewish woman who had been a NAP organizer and who subsequently married him; a close friend of mine had told me that they were sleeping together while I was still in a relationship with him — Serrette never said anything at all to me about it). In typical male leftist fashion he used sex to pit white women (in particular Jewish women) against women of color (in particular Black women) as well as to divide Black women against ourselves.

We also talked about his relationships with Lorraine Stevens and with me, and how they had impacted on my relationship with Lorraine. Serrette knew how to keep us at each other's throats, which we were for about two years. He knew our vulnerabilities: he'd play into Lorraine's victimization as a poor Black woman. And he didn't hesitate to lie: he'd call her up and tell her that I had said something critical about her (he used to call her from work every day, and speak to her for hours) and he'd tell me "bad" things she had said. I was always angry with her because I felt she should be loyal to me. It was crazy. He was using sex to manipulate both of us, even though I was sleeping with him and she wasn't. At that meeting with Fred she and I talked very openly about all of this.

Lorraine had been on the road with Serrette for a couple of months, campaigning; he had made all kinds of accusations against Fred then. (Of course, when he had the chance to raise whatever issues he wanted to at a meeting with Fred and the rest of us in New York City just before the election, he backed down. Instead, he started attacking the Black leaders of NAP for not being "strong" enough.)

At the meeting with Fred, when we described the conversations we had been having with Dennis, we realized that he had been factionalizing, that he was a liar, and that he was manipulating the hell out of all of us, especially the women.

I think Serrette hated me. He was extremely angry that while I cared a lot about him — which I did, and it wasn't a secret — I wouldn't betray NAP or Fred politically for his sake. Everything he did was very nasty because of that. I recall sitting at a table with a group of people at a party when Dennis came over to say something to one of them, who started to tell me what he had said. Dennis told her, "This is Black. Don't say it in front of Fulani." At the end of the party, he came over to me and said, "Oh, I forgot to ask you to dance." He was very vicious.

It was decided that Lorraine and I would meet with Serrette together to brief him on the meeting with Fred. That conversation, which took place in a restaurant on the Upper West Side of Manhattan, was one of the most glorious moments of my life.

He knew that we knew that for two years he had been playing us off against each other, and that we had finally gotten together, figured it out, and were there to tell him that he would never do this again. We presented a united front. At the end of it, all Serrette could say was: "If there's anything I can do, let me know." He was, first and foremost, a coward.

By meeting with him together Lorraine and I were saying to Serrette, "Back off. We've 'peeped' your cards. Never again, no matter who you're sleeping with, will you be able to manipulate us in the way that you did." Lorraine and I left the restaurant together. We were joyous; we practically jumped in the air and clicked our heels, because it felt so liberating.

Dr. Fulani...ran for Lt. Governor on the New Alliance Party line with Nancy Ross in a bid to get ballot status for the Party in 1982.

— *BLACK AMERICAN*, OCTOBER 24-30, 1985

When I first became involved in the New Alliance Party there were 10 or 12 women, several of whom were in my women's support group, who were my closest friends. I'll always be deeply indebted to them because they helped me get through the last years of my marriage. I think that when I got more political, they felt that they didn't have a place in my life anymore. But they didn't want to know what I was doing; they just couldn't understand why I wasn't trying to make it in academia, but instead was on the streets, doing demonstrations, running around with this crazy group of people who were trying to build a movement.

Gloria Strickland was different from my other friends; she came with me. She went on to become a leading member of the New Alliance Party. We had known each other since we were undergraduates at Hofstra University. I was a year ahead of her. For the first six months of her freshman year she commuted to school from her father's house, which was just a short distance from campus. Gloria would come to the Rathskeller, where all the Black students hung out, to check out the "scene." After we became friends, she told me that she used to watch me because I was always talking; she thought I had "nerve" (Gloria was shy).

We got to know each other because we were both active in the Organization of Black Collegiates. We were also both psychology majors. We used to talk about everything: how to support each other in OBC, where sexism was rampant, and in general how to deal with the men in our lives; how to educate Black kids (we were volunteer tutors); how to change the world. We went to each other's weddings and then, when we both separated from our husbands, we shared an apartment in Brooklyn for about a year. We always had a lot of fun together.

For a long time Gloria didn't want to have anything to do with NAP. She would come to events with me, but reluctantly; she wasn't really interested. Her attitude toward Fred was that he was a nice, decent person who gave good advice. Eventually all of that changed. She was working at Covenant House as a counselor to Black and Puerto Rican kids who had gotten in trouble with the law, and was being forced to confront the failure of Covenant House's liberal, do-gooder approach. And she was finding out that "star" (as she was thought of) is just the polite word for "token": her supervisors at work thought she was so smart, so nice — and a real pain in the behind whenever she said anything that challenged their way of doing things. Eventually she left Covenant House, and then it seemed that she was much more open to what I was doing. Over the years our relationship has been transformed — now we're political colleagues as well as friends. I'm very proud of the role I've played in her political development (I've pushed her to grow, intellectually and emotionally, when she thought she had gone as far as she could, or wanted to), and I'm deeply appreciative of her principledness, her loyalty, and her unswerving support for me and for our work. It means a lot to me that what she's always valued in me are those qualities that many men find hard to take: my outspokenness, my willingness to fight for what I believe in, and my self-confidence (which is sometimes taken for arrogance).

I was very opinionated, even as a child. I was fiercely, passionately determined to right the injustices and the unfairness that I knew existed in the world. And I was just as intensely confident that I — Lenora Branch from Chester, Pennsylvania — could do it, and would do it. But even so, being a Black woman leader is an extraordinary, difficult and sometimes painful enterprise.

Already Dr. Fulani has raised $1 million in federal primary matching funds...Doug Wilder raised less than $200,000 and had to drop out of the race. So when you talk about putting to-

gether a viable organization, a campaign, a political machine
— this woman has done it.

> — CATHY HUGHES, WOL RADIO [WASHINGTON, D.C.],
> FEBRUARY 1992

I like Cathy Hughes a lot. I think she's tough. She's managed
to be independent enough as a woman to call some shots in her
life. A lot of women don't have the opportunity to do that because of their dependence on men. Cathy is economically independent. She owns WOL, the hugely popular Black-oriented
station in Washington, DC. It's pretty much unheard of for a
Black woman to own her own radio station. She's very controversial. She says what's on her mind. Everybody sees her as ir-
reverent. She's completely "out of order."

The first time I remember meeting Cathy was in the summer of '88. During my first appearance on her show, she admitted that she hadn't paid any attention to me until some students had asked her why she wasn't supporting me. She apologized — and made a very strong statement regarding my accomplishments, which she's done repeatedly since then.

Cathy is one of the few Black media people, male or female, who won't hedge on the issues I raise. When I was exposing the business and political connections between Mervyn
Dymally and the Mobutu dictatorship, we talked about it. She
didn't try to speed me by it. In fact, she said Dymally should
have to account for the relationship. I also talked about Jesse
Jackson on that show, and Jesse's refusal to respond to my call
for a public debate between us during the 1992 campaign. I
wanted a dialogue between the country's leading Black
Democrat — Jesse — and the country's leading Black independent, on which path was best for the Black community. A
number of Black leaders wanted such a debate. One was Dave

Reed, the chairman of the Harold Washington Party in Chicago, who attempted to reach Jesse to set it up. Cathy Hughes also wanted a debate.

In early October of the '92 campaign, while I was waiting to go on Cathy's show, she was talking about Jesse and Jim Allen, her news director, who had accompanied Jesse to Florida. Jesse was down there demanding to know why Bush wasn't doing anything to help the people who had been devastated by Hurricane Andrew. Cathy said that if she were the president of the United States and up for re-election, and a natural disaster occurred, she would go down there, roll up her sleeves and start digging out the mud, and she would win in a landslide. How dumb could George Bush be, she asked. At that time, Black leaders who were criticizing George Bush were campaigning for the Democrats. I was sitting there thinking, "Oh, God. Jesse has her." But I needn't have worried. As soon as we went on the air, we got right into my campaign. I was concerned to make the point that what Jesse was actually doing in Florida was stumping for Bill Clinton. The next time Jesse was on her show she asked him about my campaign and why he wasn't supporting me. He was very evasive, and she picked up on that. She reminded him that I had said many times that if Jesse would take the independent political movement and build it bigger than I'm able to do, I would hand it over to him in a second and take a back seat — gladly. She asked him why he wouldn't take it from me, or support Ron Daniels, or just go independent himself. Cathy later told me — also on the air — that he was so uncomfortable he ran out of the studio after the show and forgot his hanky! That's why the community loves her — she isn't afraid to get involved in controversy. And she's not a phony.

Someone called me on the air during the campaign and

asked me if Minister Farrakhan supported me. I said to ask him. Cathy's response was to issue a challenge to the Black community. She said Black people often don't like our traditional leadership, and since we're always saying that they don't do the right thing, why do we wait to hear what they do before making our decisions? Why don't *we* direct what *they* do, she asked her listeners, by supporting me?

A Bright, Broken Promise: Washington's Marion Barry, once mockingly dubbed "Mayor for Life," sinks slowly into a quagmire of scandal, corruption and incompetence

— *TIME*, JUNE 26, 1992

Another thing I really love about Cathy is her loyalty. Her attitude is that if you're doing the right thing for the Black community, she'll support you 100%. If you're not, or if you stop, she's done with you. You could see that in her relationship to Marion Barry. Middle-class Black people hate Barry, because he was from the streets. Your stomach would recoil to hear them talk about him, they were so nasty. Cathy supported Barry. She begged him to come on the air and tell Black listeners the truth when the stories about his sexual affairs were first circulating. He said he couldn't — he made up some story about the case being in the courts and therefore he was legally prevented from talking about it. The next day he came out on a white radio show...

People think they can mess with her — the Internal Revenue Service has come after her; the Federal Communications Commission has come after her. But she gets her due from the community. She's a heroine. I feel that if she ever needs anything from me, I'll be there for her. There aren't a lot of Cathys in the world — we need more of them.

Several Black women delegates believe African-Americans have the power to make the Clinton-Gore team work in the White House by holding them accountable to the platform they endorse. "African-American people empower African-American people. Empowerment is not something the Democratic Party is ever going to give us and it's not something that anybody else is ever going to give us," said Marilyn Anderson Chase, a Boston delegate and former Paul Tsongas supporter. She said "Empowerment is something we are going to have to recognize we already have...Chase and other delegates say the party's membership is the handiwork of two-time presidential candidate Rev. Jesse Jackson.

— NEW YORK *AMSTERDAM NEWS*, JULY 18, 1992

There are so many Black women's organizations that raise money for the Democratic Party and then let the Democrats mess them over. It's such a loss. In 1992, C. Dolores Tucker, who is a founder of the National Political Caucus of Black Women, was running for Congress from Philadelphia for Bill Gray's old seat against Lucien Blackwell, a longtime member of the Black reform machine, in the Democratic Party primary. I heard that before the primary C. Dolores gave Lynn Yeakel, who was a candidate for the U.S. Senate from Pennsylvania, thousands of dollars to print palm cards with both of their pictures on them. Yeakel put C. Dolores' picture on half of them, and Blackwell's picture on the other half. When C. Dolores confronted her, Yeakel said that was how politics was done. How come C. Dolores Tucker was allowed to be humiliated like this? How come all the people that C. Dolores has worked for over the years didn't stand up for her? Someone said to me that all the talk about 1992 being "the year of the woman" really meant "the year of the white woman." They're not talking about the daughters of the women who worked on their hands and knees scrubbing the kitchen floors of well-to-do white families.

Cathy Hughes — being supportive, as always, of other Black women — had C. Dolores on her show.

C. Dolores Tucker could have held a press conference on the steps of City Hall in Philadelphia with me. She could have said, "I've been messed over by the Democratic Party for the last time. I'm going independent with Dr. Fulani." But the woman's scared to speak to me.

CHISHOLM, SHIRLEY, educator; b: Nov. 30, 1924, N.Y.C; m: Arthur Hardwick Jr.; ed: Brooklyn Coll.: B.A. (cum laude); Columbia U.: M.A.; cr: 12th Cong. Dist. NY.: U.S. representative…first woman to ever actively run for president; member of numerous civic & professional organizations including League of Women Voters, Brooklyn Br. NAACP, Delta Sigma Theta, Nat. Bd. of Americans for Dem. Action, Adv. Council, N.O.W., Hon. Com. Mem. United Negro College Fund, Natl. Assoc. Coll. Women…recipient Clairol's "Woman of Year" award for outstanding achievement in pub. affairs 1973; gallup poll's list of ten most admired women in the world 3 yrs.; recipient of numerous honorary degrees; author "Unbought & Unbossed"; "The Good Fight."

— WHO'S WHO IN BLACK AMERICA 1988

Shirley Chisholm has become a political nobody. It's kind of sad — she's living off her '60s and '70s radicalism.

Shirley's reason for founding the National Political Caucus of Black Women was that in 1984, the year that Geraldine Ferraro ended up as the vice presidential candidate of the

Democratic Party, Shirley wasn't even on Mondale's list for consideration. She founded the NPCBW as a protest. But the organization has petered out. It has no teeth.

If Shirley had endorsed me in 1988, I think that it would be a whole different ball game. After I met with her, she made a point of saying that I had a point of view which had to be heard. But she wouldn't go any further. These women are afraid that if they move with me they'll lose everything they've got. But the reality is that they're not getting much from the Democratic Party. Meanwhile, the independent political movement is clearly growing — and they're forfeiting their right to play a part in shaping it.

We have all these bright, wonderful, talented, hardworking women in the Democratic Party. They agree with what I'm doing, they'll slip me $200 in cash, but they don't want their names on my "list" because they still hope that the Democrats will give them money and recognition for their causes. They ask me if I know what it would mean for them to come out and support me. I say to them, "What in the world are you waiting around for?" They still have the irrational belief that the Democrats are going to come through for them.

Cathy Hughes is different. Whatever she does for me, she does it publicly — and she doesn't do that just for me. She takes principled stands on all kinds of controversial issues in the Black community.

If Black political women would line up with the independent political movement they would be so much stronger. If they have a shot at getting anything, they have to let the Democratic Party know that they'll leave. Women don't get anything from kissing anyone's behind — the more you do it the less you get, in politics and otherwise.

The National Organization for Women is determined that we will not go back...We will build a new political force to challenge incumbents who have abandoned the dream of equality and to challenge the unresponsive and outdated political parties. We will recruit unprecedented numbers of feminist women to run for office. We will no longer beg for our rights from men in power: we will replace them and take power ourselves.

— PATRICIA IRELAND, EXECUTIVE VICE PRESIDENT OF THE
NATIONAL ORGANIZATION FOR WOMEN

The first and only time Ellie Smeal ever responded to my request to meet with her was in 1988, when I first ran for president. I went to her office in Washington, DC — at that time she was the president of NOW — and we talked about what I was doing. My purpose in wanting to meet with her was to lay out the 1988 campaign and to ask for her support.

What I most remember about the meeting with Ellie is that we talked a lot about ballot status. That's the basis for the leaders of the women's movement to have a positive dialogue with me — it's a "safe" topic. We've never had a frank discussion about the role of the women's movement in this country relative to the women I represent — women of color, poor women and independent women, or about whatever conflicts and questions they have concerning NAP, or about NOW's relationship to the Democratic Party.

I went to NOW's 1988 annual convention in Buffalo some time after the meeting with Ellie. I had asked for the opportunity to address the convention, but had been turned down. However, Pat Ireland, who was a vice president of NOW at the time, quietly told my deputy campaign manager, Jackie Salit, that there were provisions in the NOW by-laws to collect petition signatures to bring a resolution to the floor. We went with Pat's suggestion, and hundreds of women — more than 50% of the delegates in attendance at the convention — signed a petition calling on NOW to acknowledge the historic significance of my campaign and to assume responsibility for letting every woman in the United States know that an independent, progressive Black woman would be on the ballot in every state and the District of Columbia. Despite the support of the rank and file, however, the leadership ignored the petition. It was tabled for review by the national executive board, but never acted upon. Yet while the national office stonewalled the campaign, I spoke at the NOW state conventions in California and in Florida and, particularly in California, received a lot of support. The rank and file was definitely interested in independent politics. That was why, in 1989, NOW's leaders bowed to the pressure from its membership and formed the Commission for a Responsible Democracy to investigate the viability of a third party in America. Three years later the Commission recommended that the NOW convention endorse the founding of the 21st Century Party, a move which was enthusiastically supported by the rank and file.

When I walked into the 21st Century Party Convention — which was held in Washington on the last weekend of September 1992 — I think people weren't sure why I was there or what I was going to do. I went because that party is as much mine as anyone else's in this country. I'm concerned about its growth and development because I think that women need to kick — not kiss — the Democratic Party goodbye and build something independent.

I'm proud of the women who are taking the lead in building the 21st Century Party. One reason I've been so angry with feminists is that there are so many passionate, powerful, smart, wonderful women like the ones who were in that room — women who have the guts to break with the status quo and stand up for women's rights — but the leadership is so conservatized by their relationship to the Democratic Party that although they say all the right things they screw it up; they won't move. I've felt that very strongly as a woman of color. These women *say* they're going to do the right thing — and then they end up voting for "feminists" like Bill Clinton!

Ellie ran the convention. This was the first time I've ever seen her in action that close up. People love her. They have a lot of respect for her. She's very smart. And she's a leader. You couldn't miss that. I understand why people follow her. I hope she leads them very passionately out of the Democratic Party.

I went up to the dais to say hello to Ellie and to Dolores Huerta. It was the first time I had met Dolores, although we'd spoken a few times on the phone. She knew who I was and was very friendly. I had invited her to NAP's convention, which took place the week before; Dolores said she was overwhelmed by all the things she had to do to get ready for the 21st Century Party Convention. She wasn't saying no; just that she couldn't make it this time. She sent a telegram expressing her support. We'll keep inviting her.

I went to a workshop on ballot access, which representatives of the Rainbow Lobby also attended. NAP and the Rainbow Lobby have done a *lot* of work on ballot access, and people listened to what we had to say very attentively: by and large, neither the left nor the women associated with NOW have done much in the way of independent politics. So we were able to teach them what we know without getting bogged down in the differences between us and them. We lobbied for the Fair Elections Bill, which would break down some of the barriers to participatory democracy and inclusion by standardizing voter registration and ballot-access requirements, and for the Democracy in Presidential Debates Act, which would require presidential candidates who receive public funding to participate in debates sponsored by a non-partisan organization and would include significant independent candidates; this is legislation which they can support — and they did.

I went there to teach. Even with all the pretense that we don't exist, that we're not authentic independents, the fact is that we've been out there on the streets and in the courts for the last 15 years; we have some expertise and I want to give it — even if they don't acknowledge that it's coming from me. There's a lot more at stake than whether they send me flowers or not — which I don't have to worry about, because they won't!

Margaret Hagelin, who is married to John Hagelin, was at the convention to talk about what the Natural Law Party is doing. But they didn't let her; it was very controlled, to keep people — in particular, me — from speaking. But I introduced Margaret to Ellie as a way of saying to NOW, "We're here, and we're not going anywhere. There are other independent forces in this country, and in order for this to get off the ground you have to relate to them. You can't ignore them, and you can't ignore us." Ellie was cordial to Margaret, and asked her what the Natural Law Party was about.

There were moments during the founding convention of the 21st Century Party that weekend when I felt such overwhelming passion for the women in that room. Some of them had grey hair, some of them had gotten all dressed up…these were women who had the guts to go up against the patriarchy, despite the cost.

At the end of the convention I told Ellie that I was glad to be there and glad to be a member and that if there was anything I could do I'm available.

If NOW continues to build this party — and I think it has the potential to grow, it has a natural constituency, people are down for it — then NOW and NAP *will* work together, because they don't have a choice. We are out here, and if they're serious about taking on the two-party status quo they have to rely on other people — even if they don't agree with us 100% — who are also fighting like hell to advance the cause of independent politics.

So I look forward to working with Ellie. Even though we're not friends, we sort of broke through the distance between us. I'm not saying that now when I call her up she's definitely going to call me back — but she might.

I think that NOW is used to relating to Black women, Latina women, Asian American women and Native American women as tokens. I've always refused to participate in what I consider to be a fake "dialogue" — which they conduct every year — on how to get more women of color to join the organization. If you want more women of color to join NOW then you do the same thing that you do to get white women to join — you go to wherever they are and you organize them. If you're not doing that then you won't have them in your organization. And if you're not doing that then it's a statement about how much you want them.

What NOW brings to the table is a primarily white and middle-class feminist movement — including, to some degree, middle-class lesbians. What I bring to the table is a relationship to working-class women, particularly women of color, and an intimate involvement in the life of this country's communities of color. If the leaders of the 21st Century Party really are serious about building a relationship to women of color, they can't bypass me.

Ellie has kept her distance from me. I don't think she's going to be able to maintain that distance and build what she wants to build. At some point, if we're going to have a real independent political movement in America, she and I are going to have to sit down at the table together and work. I think we've begun that process, and I'm eager to do what I can do for the 21st Century Party in New York City and New York state. That's why I joined it: I'm going to be active.

That man over there says that women need to be helped into carriages and lifted over ditches — and to have the best place everywhere.

Nobody ever helps me into carriages or over mud-puddles — or gives me the best place at the table!

And ain't I a woman? Look at me! Look at my arm! I have ploughed and planted and gathered into barns, and no man could get ahead of me! And ain't I a woman?

I could work as much and eat as much as a man — when I could get it — and bear the lash as well! And ain't I a woman?

— SOJOURNER TRUTH

Fred often urges me to perform the part of a political leader. I used to think of performing as being phony, and I wanted to be "genuine." But to be "natural" would be to act out the social role in which I've been "cast" as a Black woman, who is either a victim, a token, a Black bitch or all three. So I perform the historic role I'm needed to play: a powerful African American woman leader, and I play it to the hilt. Stepping outside the accepted social role of a Black woman is a performance. I feel less anxious when I do it. The more I come out, the more all kinds of people come out with me.

As a Black woman running for president for the first time, back in 1988, I even had to prove that I could speak. In the first moments of every TV show I was on I used to be terrified that I'd make a mistake. In 1992 I didn't have to prove myself in the same way.

Recently, a new supporter said to me, "I think what you're doing is great. Too bad that you're Black and a woman." She thought that if I were a white man I could be more powerful. But what I'm doing is what only a Black woman can do; it's not coincidental that the spokesperson for the Black-led independent political movement we're building "turned out" to be me. Jesse Jackson didn't want the part. My history, who I am in the world, makes me the person to make *this* statement. I'm very different from the white men who've been president of the United States. Increasingly, all kinds of people are saying to this Black woman: "I don't give a damn who you are — I like what you're doing. Keep doing it, Sister."

"Don't worry," I tell them. "I am."

Photo credits

Other books available from Castillo International

Independent Black Leadership in America

The Man Behind the Sound Bite:
The Real Story of the Rev. Al Sharpton

The Myth of Psychology